The Last Boat Home

Robert E. Lee

A.H. STOCKWELL
PUBLISHERS SINCE 1898

First published in 2006
This edition published in 2023 by
Robert E. Lee
in association with
Arthur H Stockwell Ltd
West Wing Studios
Unit 166, The Mall
Luton, Bedfordshire
ahstockwell.co.uk

Contents

Foreword v

Prologue vii

Chapter I 1

Chapter II 10

Chapter III 21

Chapter IV 30

Chapter V 33

Chapter VI 38

Chapter VII 41

Chapter VIII 44

Chapter IX 47

Chapter X 56

Chapter XI 59

Chapter XII 64

Chapter XIII 68

Tribute: The Royal Engineers 74

Foreword

Carol Lee adores her ninety-year-old father but is still in awe of him, a North Devonian of strong character who has no time for fools. From childhood she has been intrigued by the snippets she has heard over the years about his service during the Second World War, which have come up periodically in family conversation. Her husband, Sergeant 'Bob' Lee, a highly respected police officer in charge of North Devon's traffic police, felt that Carol's father had a story that ought to be told and not lost to posterity. He spent many hours talking to Gil and patiently recorded the story of this 'ordinary' man who, when the crunch came, acted in the finest traditions of the Corps of Royal Engineers. Sapper Gilbert James Mock joined the Army as a volunteer in December 1939 and left the Army, still a sapper, at the end of the war – his promotion prospects blunted by his outspoken criticism of some of his peers and an aversion to the finer points of military discipline. A short fuse is never an asset to a sapper, whatever the circumstances!

Many books and articles have been written about the overwhelming odds faced by the British Expeditionary Force in their retreat to the French coast and eventual evacuation over the beaches at Dunkirk; and many brave acts and tragedies took place during this desperate time for the British Army. History records that, in order to delay the German Army's ruthless advance, holding forces were deployed, including small teams of sappers whose task was to blow up bridges, lay mines and destroy roads to delay the enemy advance. Although from an Artisan Works Company, Gil was a volunteer who was tasked with the vital job of blowing up a bridge. No planned escape route was possible for the sappers and their escorting platoon of infantry in this desperate situation. They were on their own with no hope of evacuation through Dunkirk. This story is not written by a general, a war correspondent or professional author; it records in simple language the events experienced by a sapper – a very brave Braunton boy.

Colonel R. C. Gilliat (retired), late RE

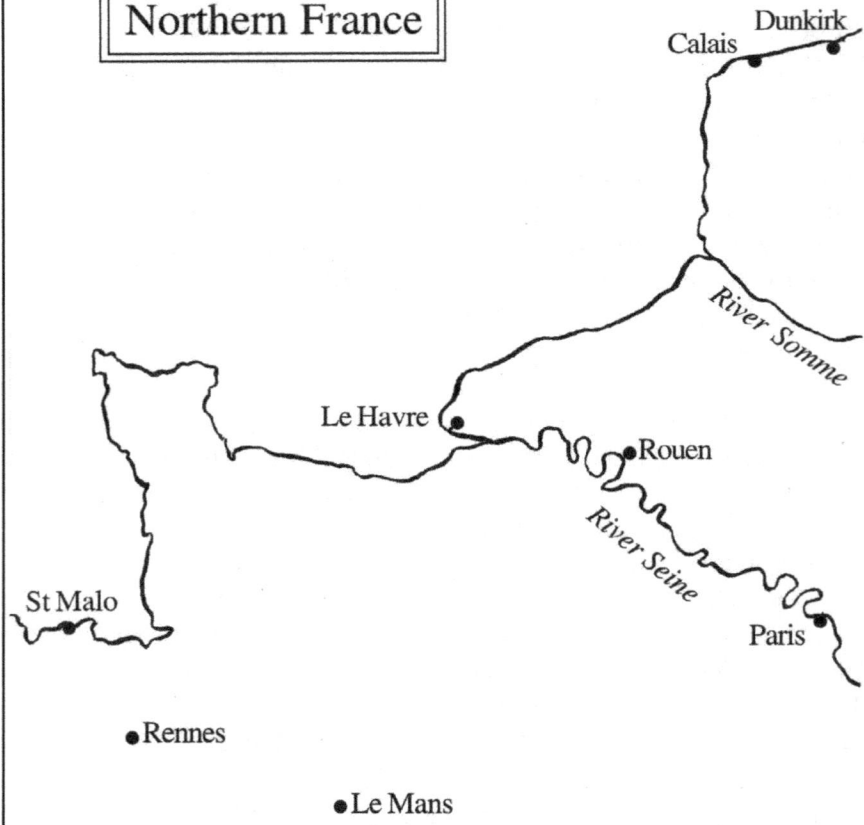

Northern France

Calais Dunkirk

River Somme

Le Havre Rouen

River Seine

St Malo Paris

Rennes

Le Mans

Prologue

What is it about the evacuation of France in 1940 that fascinates people? The men who survived and their families have mixed emotions. For others, it is just a chapter in European history they find interesting, or not. With the passage of time many don't care, or are ignorant of the historical significance. Whatever your view on the subject, there is one overarching, indisputable fact, that had it not been for the actions of *extra*ordinary men and women, in whatever role they found themselves during late May/early June 1940, the map of Europe and our way of life could be far removed from that which we enjoy today.

This is the story of just one of those *extra*ordinary people. His personal experiences and opinions formed during the chaos that focused on a small seaside town called Dunkirk, from where an estimated 338,226 Allied troops were evacuated to England. In reality, the whole coastline of northern France became an escape route, so the total number was higher than that. It was a crucial turning point during the Second World War – in the words of Winston Churchill, 'a miracle of deliverance'.

The consensus amongst rank-and-file Tommies desperately trying to hold the line, was that the 'red bands' (staff officers), of whatever status, were reliving 1914–18. They expected the Allies to hold up the German advance and dig in, when it was plain to the fighting men that our leaders had learnt nothing from recent events. Blitzkrieg, the new military shock-and-awe tactic, used with such devastating effect against our friends in Poland and the Low Countries, could soon be unleashed on France. The Allies faced a ruthless, highly disciplined and confident military machine, strong and experienced in modern battlefield tactics, including recent veterans of the Spanish Civil War. By May 1940 the Germans had found a winning formula, using methods that abandoned the perceived rules of engagement to feed the Nazis' perverse brand of National Socialist egotism.

Ordinary Germans were most likely of the belief their military campaigns were in pursuit of national pride and security, to regain the lands and reunite people exiled following the carnage of the First World War. But of course it did not stop there and our political leaders naively allowed that to happen. Consequently Great Britain was not ready for another world war.

So it was in the spring of 1940 when the lions of the BEF awaited the inevitable invasion of France. Within their perception, the 'red bands' and politicians had seen to it that Dunkirk was, quite simply, waiting to happen – echoes of 1914–18, lions led by donkeys yet again.

This book is written in a style to recount, as faithfully as possible, Gil Mock's real-life experience and to try to capture something of the atmosphere. There are no vainglorious frills, just an honest recollection of personal thoughts and actions from over sixty years ago. To set the scene and put events into context, some general history has been included, but continual fatigue and the emergency of the ordeal meant that days had a way of merging into one another. No matter how much detail has been lost over time, the raw emotion can soon well to the surface. One can see it in his eyes – Gil is back there, trying to make sense of it all, still fighting and looking to deliver a bloody nose to a 'red band'.

This is an *extra*ordinary soldier's unique tribute to the Royal Engineers and all those caught up in conflict, wherever and whenever that may be – especially if their feet hurt!

Chapter I

"Chop his legs!" "Come on, Gil, get 'im!" and other equally endearing, but not so delicately worded, shouts of encouragement went up from the pals, during one of the regular soccer matches played at Bridestowe, near Okehampton, Devon, in the August of 1941. Such was the esteem in which Sergeant Major Jennings was held by his sappers, that at every opportunity less than polite gentlemanly requests were made of their most fiery comrade to have a pop at the beloved senior NCO, and he did. In one memorable game, Sapper 1910766 Gilbert James Mock, Royal Engineers, playing in the fullback position, delivered any number of his, by now, infamous shoulder charges, sending the hapless NCO poleaxed to the turf each time. The cheers were deafening. Gil was a hero to his pals and subsequently the cookhouse staff, with whom, as a result, he spent several hours peeling spuds!

Thanks to the confusion of war and the suppression of information, it was not common knowledge in 1940, nor sadly do the majority appreciate now, just how many hundreds of thousands of Allied servicemen who managed to escape northern France, owed their lives to a few unsuspecting but nevertheless heroic fullbacks like Gil – men the War Office had written off as dead, having been left behind in France to hold up or at least frustrate the German advance.

Gilbert James Mock, Gil to friends and family, was born in the village of Braunton, in North Devon, on the 23rd October 1915. The second of four children, he was the product of an austere Edwardian age, in which loyalty to family and Empire were drummed into you. The First World War was of course raging at the time. This strict upbringing was to produce a generally quiet, vulnerable lad, but trapped within was a volcanic temper and his boyhood friends knew which buttons to press

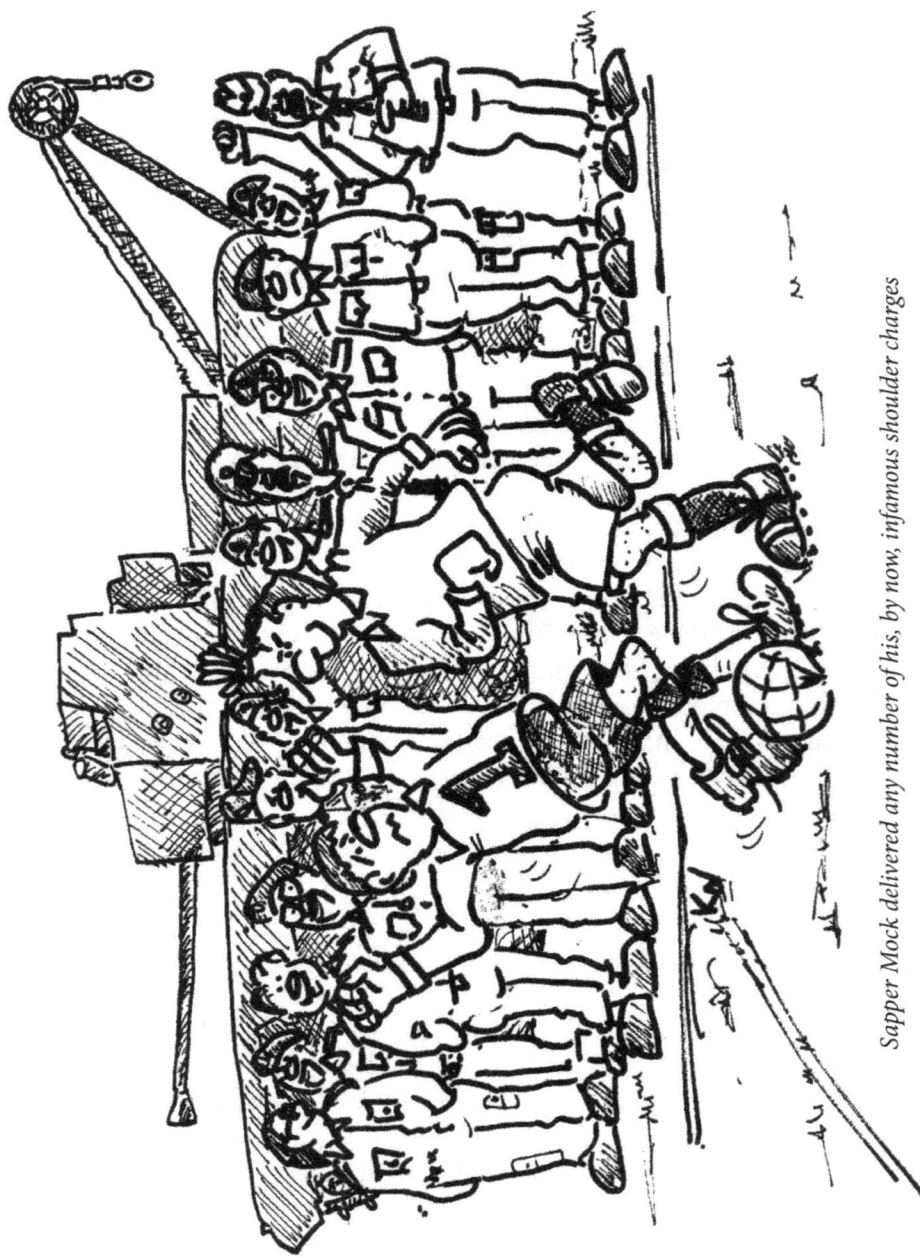

Sapper Mock delivered any number of his, by now, infamous shoulder charges

to make him explode with rage; they then just stood back and enjoyed the performance.

Even to this day, beyond his ninetieth year, temper can occasionally get the better of him. Raising his walking stick high above his head, and then with a swift downward swipe, the old soldier simulates what he would do to any annoying skateboarder, or cyclist threatening to bump into him on the footpath. But the worst horrors he reserves for potential muggers, burglars, terrorists or similar villainous types, like doorbell ringers! His punishment would then lean more toward bayonet drill and disembowelment.

On leaving school his academic achievements were average, but he was a man of action, not letters, and things were about to change. Apprenticed to the building trade, Gil proved to be a natural craftsman and was to rapidly earn a reputation for the quality of his work. Brick- and block-laying, plastering, carpentry, roof tiling, etc.: whatever he was taught he mastered. He attributes these practical skills to inheritance from his father, who for many years was foreman at a cane-basket factory in Braunton.

Gil grew up with a fascination for the countryside, spending many childhood hours playing on the three-hundred-and-sixty-acre Braunton Great Field, a natural wetland wilderness of fields, hedgerows, marsh and streams, supporting a diverse range of wildlife. It is a famous archaeological site that remains a rare example of medieval strip farming.

Beyond that, toward the sea, is Braunton Burrows, a National Nature Reserve boasting the largest system of sand dunes in the United Kingdom, covering 970 hectares (2,397 acres), stretching over six kilometres (four miles) along the shore and two kilometres (one and a quarter miles) inland. Rich in flora and fauna, this is now a UNESCO Biosphere Reserve. After 1940 the area was to become an important training ground for D-Day and the Second Front, and is, somewhat controversially, still favoured today for military training, with 603 hectares being leased to the Ministry of Defence.

The dunes then flatten out to form an idyllic three-mile-long golden sandy beach, called Saunton Sands, very popular with tourists and locals alike, and also film and television producers. The outstanding natural beauty of the sands stretches along the shoreline far into the distance.

Not one to miss a financial opportunity, even in his tender years, Gil would spend many a rewarding hour earning extra pocket money caddying for the well heeled at Saunton Golf Club, with its eighteen-hole championship-standard links courses. The West Course, built in the mid-thirties, was to be lost as a battle training ground during the Second World War. Here American troops practised for the Normandy Landings, which resulted in much damage to the dunes and severe erosion.

Throughout childhood and into adolescence the pedal cycle was this boy racer's mode of transport. At that time road safety was nowhere near the issue it is today. Privately owned motor vehicles were rare between the two world wars, especially in rural areas such as North Devon. Then it was possible to ride the six miles between Braunton and Barnstaple during the daytime and not see one vehicle.

The combination of outdoor work and heavy labour, on various building projects, saw his six-foot-three-inch frame develop a muscular physique. He had blue eyes, light-brown hair and he was considered, mainly by himself, of course, to be quite a handsome young man. His only vice was tobacco and he was rarely seen without a smouldering pipe in his mouth – a habit he would enjoy for almost forty years.

The pattern of daily life took a familiar routine, until one memorable day. On a trip with friends to the beach at Saunton Sands, he met Beryl Knight, a lively, vivacious girl, three years his junior. She was a Barnstaple girl and in character the total opposite to his quiet, shy persona – just what he needed. Despite all odds, the relationship grew, slowly at first, in keeping with the general pace of life at that time. But the bond between them was to endure, not only family hostility from both sides, but the unforeseen challenges yet to unfold. Over sixty-five years later they remain dedicated to one another.

News reports on the wireless grew increasingly dark. In March 1938, in blatant violation of the Treaty of Versailles, Hitler marched his troops into the city of Vienna, to an enthusiastic welcome from the Austrian people. That same year, no doubt fearing for the safety of their own countries, the French and then the British premier, Neville Chamberlain, followed a misguided policy of appeasement toward Hitler and ceded the Sudetenland to Germany. After the fall of Czechoslovakia and the blitzkrieg unleashed on Poland, the rest of Europe waited for the Third Reich to spread its wings. In September 1939 the British Empire declared war on Nazi Germany. The familiar, pastoral ways of old England were about to change for ever, and sleepy North Devon would not escape the rude awakening.

Employment opportunities during the pre-war years were pretty bleak. However, he was working on a building project at Croyde Holiday Camp, when in early December 1939, Gil answered the call to arms. A newspaper advertisement was asking for tradesmen to join the Army, promising the princely wage of six shillings and sixpence a day. So off to the recruiting office, situated in the post office sorting rooms in Cross Street, Barnstaple, went he and four other young Braunton lads – Harry Irwin, Eddy Stanton, Jack Woolaway and Jack Perryman. There they met a lad from Ilfracombe and another lad, called Ansell, from South Molton. All these likely lads were in the building trades and eager to do their bit!

After a very brief interview and an even less detailed medical later, during which an Army doctor told Gil what he already knew – that, in simple terms, his feet were not good. However, the doctor promised if they became worse the Army would give him suitable work. Little did he know what that would mean! He was then promptly given an inappropriate A1 medical grade and volunteered his numerous practical skills, enlisting with the Royal Engineers. The officer in charge tried to persuade Gil to join the Brigade of Guards, but engineering was an obvious choice for the strapping young tradesman with dodgy feet. In fact, all seven new pals were to join the sappers that day.

Meeting on the platform of Barnstaple Railway Station just a few weeks later, the seven pals said their fond farewells to friends and family and, with mixed emotions, boarded the Waterloo train. Beryl wished them all good fortune and waved as the train pulled out. After an unremarkable journey, which took them via Exeter and Salisbury, they had plenty of time to reflect upon what the future might hold in store. On reaching London, they changed trains, continuing the journey east, and eventually the pals reported for duty at Kitchener Barracks, in Chatham, Kent.

They arrived at the Royal Engineers' home base depot, in Chatham, on the 11th January 1940 and were soon to understand the meaning of 'basic training'. That is exactly what each new intake of 250 recruits received, and once a fortnight another new company passed out. Men from all walks of life were brought together, with many a pardon being granted to convicted felons who chose to serve out their sentence in uniform. One of these ex-cons was a particularly uncouth chap, with a vocabulary to match, who found it impossible to speak the King's English without turning the air blue. He was a real bad lad and one to watch, but he wasn't to bother Gil, who soon proved his physical abilities.

Bayonet practice followed, comprising static drills, defensive postures and blood-curdling screams of "Arghhh!"

The first port of call for the new pals was the quartermaster's store. Here they were roughly measured for a uniform, albeit no tape measure in sight. With numerous items of equipment and clothing balanced on outstretched arms, they later emerged somewhat dazed. Not quite Savile Row! Just what did the sergeant mean, "It'll fit where it touches"? Oh well, it's all free!

The next call was another very swift medical, with exactly the same comments about his feet as received back in Barnstaple, resulting in yet another inappropriate Al grade and the promise of the mysterious 'suitable work'. But this medical was different, for it included that all-time favourite, inoculations. Against what, they were never told. The inoculations must have been good, though, judging by the fire-extinguisher proportions of the syringe and the javelin for a needle. Proof of the mixture's potency came the next day, when every last man went down with flu-type symptoms. Not that the Army gave a damn of course – no compassion was shown whatsoever. Nothing was to delay their training.

Then it was off to the armoury, where each man was issued his very own .303 Lee–Enfield rifle, all of which were 1914 vintage, brought out of mothballs in defence of the Empire again – well, once degreased and cleaned up, that is. This rifle and a fearsome-looking eighteen-inch bayonet, were to be Gil's constant companions throughout the next six years of Army service.

Each basic course comprised of little else but square-bashing and very simple weapon-cleaning instruction. The lads did eventually receive one whole day on a shooting range, to learn which end of their rifle the bullets came out of, and after all of twenty precious rounds of ammunition, they were declared competent. Really? Well, no one was killed or injured in their platoon through friendly fire, so that was deemed a result! Bayonet practice followed, comprising static drills, defensive postures, yelling "On guard!" then a few hops and a skip, and a blood-curdling scream of "Arghhh!" whilst venomously skewering some inanimate sandbags. After this they were declared competent, again. At that time the only thing Gil felt truly competent at was his ability to throw his bayonet from anything up to fifteen feet and consistently hit the centre of whatever he was aiming at. For a betting man this skill was a nice little earner!

Their instructors had all been Territorial soldiers before the war, and the plan was for these men to stay with the platoon they taught and become their NCOs. So every new intake of recruits had different trainers.

7

Standards were very much dependent on the enthusiasm and instructional skills of individual ex-Terriers, who only had one dedicated go at teaching, but tried to make up for it afterwards with on-the-job instruction along the way. Throughout their training one of the sergeants constantly drummed a cheerful message into the pals: "When in the field, don't stop to pick up wounded!"

The pals were only in barracks for the first week of basic training. Just before a new intake of recruits arrived, the previous group were moved out of camp and into civilian lodgings. There simply wasn't enough room for them all. There were two men to a lodging. Gil and one other sapper shared a room in a modest terraced house owned by a married couple in their fifties. All 250 pals were in similar room-only accommodation, within a few hundred yards of Luton Arches railway bridge. All meals were taken at the barracks.

Each morning of the second week, the pals mustered for a roll-call under Luton Arches, before marching the mile or so back to camp. Air raids on the nearby docks were a constant reminder of the national emergency rapidly escalating.

Gil soon became used to living full-time in uniform, but found the best part was the food. With the war in its infancy, rationing had not started and the Army diet suited him well.

At the end of two weeks they were given a forty-eight-hour home-leave pass and rail warrant. But when the North Devon pals reached home there was barely enough time for Gil to drink a cup of tea, tell his parents and Beryl what he had been up to (well, almost everything!) before catching the next train back to Chatham.

On return to barracks, the newly formed 670th Artesian Works Company, Royal Engineers, gathered up all their kit, brushed and pressed those 'expertly tailored Savile Row' uniforms as best they could, then stepped onto the parade ground, where, to the stirring sound of the Royal Engineers' military band they passed out as supposedly trained soldiers. This reflected, as they knew later, the desperate but costly game of catch-up our national leaders were playing, pouring reservists and ill-trained volunteer troops across the Channel, to redress the earlier naive belief in and subsequent collapse of Neville Chamberlain's 'Peace for our time' pledge.

The proud pals, rifles at the slope, then followed the band out of the barrack gates with bugles, drums and flutes playing, as they all marched down to Chatham Railway Station, amid cheers from passers-by and well-wishers. Even the chaps who during training had insisted on swinging their right arm with their right leg, a totally unnatural action, got it right on the day. They then boarded a train bound for Southampton Docks and embarkation for duty with the British Expeditionary Force (BEF) in France.

Chapter II

On or about the 27th January 1940, the pals from Kitchener Barracks arrived at Southampton Docks, where they boarded a former peacetime ferry and 'enjoyed' a rough-weather crossing to Le Havre. Gil found a spot inside the crowded ship, roughly amidships, where the rolling was not so exaggerated. He still felt awful but managed not to throw up, finding it beneficial to remain standing throughout the three-hour crossing. It was about that time when he made the conscious decision not to make good friends with anyone, just in case they didn't make it. He could then concentrate on looking after himself. Apart from that, he was to be constantly on the move, working with different men on various projects at numerous locations, which made it easier to achieve.

Landing on the north coast of France, the eager pals had no time to find their land legs before, together with their ex-training staff who were now substantive NCOs, they were all herded into railway cattle trucks for an eighty-mile journey east to Forges-les-Eaux, which in turn is about fifty miles north-east of Rouen, near a spa with mineral works, known then as the Crystal Fountain. Of historical interest, it had also been the tragic crash site of the airship R101 back in October 1930.

There, in the middle of a forest, 670th Artesian Works Company spent just over four months putting their trade skills to good use, building a huge military transit camp, comprising barracks, other ancillary buildings and a single-track concrete road right through the middle. As the name Artesian suggests, one of the company's main tasks was to secure clean water sources, and many a day was spent clearing and then placing pumps and structures to enable water extraction from local streams. Of course, pollution was not an issue then as it is today, so purification was easy. The company also had borehole-drilling equipment, but Gil never saw it being used. They were also sent, for a few days at a time, to smaller camps dotted around the countryside, completing a variety of building jobs.

Gil's pipe was almost continuously burning – apart from on the parade ground, that is, although he had considered marching out with it once, until a mental picture of the sergeant major pulling it from his mouth, with Gil's false teeth still clenched to the end of the stem, and then stamping all over the lot made him see sense. The trouble was that advertisements suggested tobacco was good for you. It was issued as an Army ration in France, and for some it was valued more than food. The non-smokers still drew their tobacco entitlement to sell on, and if the ration failed to turn up for any reason there was hell up in the camp. Gil's consumption of tobacco was so prodigious that Beryl also sent regular top-up supplies by post.

One fine spring day, whilst working on secondment, installing an incinerator at a small military camp a few miles from Forges-les-Eaux, Gil and a group of work pals were enjoying a short lunch break, lying on a grassy riverbank eating pies and drinking tea. He had just lit up a cigarette to give his pipe a five-minute rest, when suddenly he felt a sharp pain to the little finger of his outstretched left hand. Uttering a few choice expletives, he saw a small unidentified snake, about finger width and twelve inches long, slithering away into the undergrowth.

Uttering a few choice expletives, he saw a small unidentified snake

Quick as a flash, in true Western cowboy style, he began to suck at the puncture wound to draw the venom out. It only took five minutes to reach the field medical unit, but in that short time the back of his hand and wrist had swollen up alarmingly. Even more unnerving for Gil, the medical officer had to refer to a book before deciding on how to deal with it! But, in fairness, no one knew the species of this venomous villain.

The next day things were decidedly worse, so the MO sent him to an Army dressing station – one hut with a few beds therein. Here they cheerfully announced they had no antidote! So his left arm was swathed from wrist to elbow in an absorbent kaolin poultice.

The third day saw a large lump appear in his armpit and each time the poultice was changed he had to sit with his arm in a bowl of hot water. It took about a week for the lump to disappear, at which time he returned to his unit.

In late May 1940, Operation Dynamo, the evacuation of the BEF and her Allies via a bridgehead at Dunkirk started. Three companies of RE, about seven hundred men in total, based in and around Forges-les-Eaux, were placed on standby to move north toward Dunkirk and the Belgian border, but not told why. This time the Army went soft, promising to transport them by lorry instead of railway cattle truck.

Unbeknown to the pals, and with best British understatement, when the balloon went up things did not go too well for the Allies. By the 22nd May, General Heinz Guderian's XIX Corps, which was comprised of the 1st, 2nd and 10th Panzer Divisions, had swept all before them and reached the north coast at Abbeville. So quickly had this happened that the bewildered French civilians thought the blond, dusty warriors must be Dutch, or English. Even the OKW, the German high command, had not planned what to do next.

Fortunately for Gil, the German XIX Corps received orders to sweep north and seize the Channel ports of Boulogne, Calais and Dunkirk. In one day alone the panzers advanced forty miles and, in no time at all, the well-documented horrors and heroism of Dunkirk started to unfold.

For three weeks, the seven hundred sappers were deliberately held in reserve. The pals continued to complete their routine jobs, whilst small snippets of glum news filtered in. They were given no official briefings and were told nothing about Dunkirk. Throughout those confusing days they often watched, in no little bewilderment, as their BEF colleagues, accompanied by units from the French and what seemed like the entire Belgian Army, who, unbeknown to the pals, had formerly surrendered on the 28th May, streamed past in full retreat.

"Can we go with them, Sarge?" was an oft-heard request, to which, in typical Army style, the reply was always blunt and predictable, roughly translated from Anglo-Saxon to read, "No."

The pals started to get an inkling something was about to happen when they were marched off to the firing range. For only the second time since enlisting, a sergeant assisted them to sight their rifles, and they loosed a few practice rounds. Whilst there, twelve German aircraft flew down the valley near the camp, dropping bombs on troops moving along the roads. Two aircraft broke away and dived on the petrol storage tanks and ammunition dumps, scoring direct hits and sending both targets up in flames and explosions. The pals had nothing but their rifles to shoot back with, and the gesture of defiance was futile.

The pals had nothing but their rifles to shoot back with

13

However, a short time later, Gil was to fire his rifle whilst not on a shooting range. Taking his turn on guard duty at the Forges-les-Eaux perimeter fence one dark night, the usual noises and figments of the imagination were playing their customary tricks. This is a strange phenomenon to which anyone who has worked alone and outside through the night can attest – even more so in this case, given the uncertainty of Gil's situation. Having every intention of shooting first, Gil put a round into the breach of his 1914 rifle and slammed the bolt home. Unfortunately the safety catch had malfunctioned, so when he moved his hand back an itchy finger caught the trigger and bang! a .303 round went skywards.

The sergeant major reacted instantly and turned out the rest of the guard, who made an impressive show of strength. No doubt the local wildlife decided not to venture out again that night. Thinking on his feet, Gil reported hearing someone in the bushes, so he had taken no chances and fired a warning shot! A little exaggeration, perhaps, but no harm was done and he got away with it. Two days later the quartermaster sergeant confirmed the safety catch on his rifle was faulty and tried to fix it, but the catch was always to be suspect and Gil learnt not to trust it.

On the 12th June, some eight days after the last Allied soldier was lifted from the beach at Dunkirk, whilst still at Forges-les-Eaux, Gil took the opportunity to send Beryl a Field Service Post Card (Army form 2042), containing a bland, strictly censored message, confirming he was all right. Handed to the sergeant and officer who regularly collected the post, it was to be several days later, somewhere around the 25th June, that Beryl received the card which remarkably they still have.

The very next day, the 13th June, 250 sappers from the company, about a third of those being held in reserve, were sent north-east toward the German lines on the River Somme, of First World War infamy. As promised, the pals were spoilt, travelling the 120 miles, not in railway cattle trucks, but by 'luxury' boneshaking Army lorry. This was to be a demolition job on a mammoth scale across a 100-mile front, stretching from the coast at Abbeville, toward the Belgian border, in a belated attempt at guarding Paris and, as they were soon to discover, their own retreat.

Preparations for their pyrotechnic task started immediately on arrival at St Valery, where all 250 of them gathered around a bridge just outside the town. There they received a brief introduction to explosives, albeit one or two of the ex-con bad lads demonstrated uncanny ability! Technically, Gil found it simple; charges were placed in strategic structural places, electric wire inserted and laid. Just one small hitch: Due to an oversight by a 'red band', there were not enough batteries for the firing systems, so the electric cable on most of the 100 bridges had to be completely replaced with a safety fuse (which can be lit with a match) connected to detonators. Anyway, after several hours' hard work at the demonstration site, and numerous bowls of pipe tobacco later, the instructions for detonation continued, with the simple sequence of: strike match, wait for the safety fuse to smoke and fizz, then run!

The training intensified. Next on their 'hit list' was a single-track, iron girder-construction railway bridge leading west out of St Valery. Although not part of any main-line system, it still presented the Germans with a Somme crossing point. The men were split into three teams, each led by a staff-sergeant instructor who hurriedly attempted to teach them the rudiments of hand-firing, fuse-laying, gun-cotton uses, primer and detonator construction, and dynamics. Three years of college was condensed into one hour in the field – sounds about right!

Gil and his team of forty engineers marched off to the railway bridge, where they dug holes in the ballast underneath two sections of track at the seating point, where the bridge meets the land. One tin of amatol was carefully placed in each hole and a detonator clipped to each fuse. Again, it was all hand-firing because there were no batteries. Once the men had retired about three hundred yards the one-and-a-half-minute fuse was lit as the instructor sprinted to join them.

Throughout all this frantic training the inexorable noise of battle could be heard approaching, so when their new-laid explosives went up, it eerily blended with the background tumult.

A bizarre sight befell them as the two sections of rail track, still attached to the majority of their sleepers, along with tons of ballast, rose about one hundred feet into the air, and appeared to hover for a second or two before crashing back down to earth in a twisted heap. Transfixed by this spectacle, the team watched from what they thought to be a safe distance. However, a large wayward lump of sleeper was secretly winging its way toward them and without warning it landed squarely on the man standing immediately next to Gil. Everyone instinctively ducked and Gil's heart missed a beat, but the only damage was a two-inch dent in the chap's tin helmet. The sergeant, sympathetic as ever, reminded them, "An Engineer's head is full of concrete, and a good job too." Whilst all around expressed their relief by laughing heartily, the fortunate sapper in question demonstrated his copious repertoire of obscenities.

The chosen few were then split up into teams of three and assigned a bridge somewhere on the River Somme stretching about one hundred miles east. The instructions were to blow the bridge, then make their way east along the river valley. Gil and two other sappers were amongst the first to be posted, being sent to a small single-track bridge, measuring about fifteen-foot wide by seventy-foot long, made entirely of concrete, which stood near the town of St Valery.

They were escorted by an officer and his platoon of forty tough Cameron Highlanders, who, by the way, were the last British regiment to wear kilts in action. This was against regulations, but it summed up the defiant mood within the ranks at that time.

Meanwhile the 500 sappers of 670th Artesian Works Company fortunate enough not to have been moved to the front line were sent home, probably via St Malo, from where they were amongst the 21,000 officially recorded as being evacuated on the 16th and 17th June. On arrival in Blighty, these men were posted to Leeds. The top brass had already written off Gil and the sappers assigned to the Somme bridges, so the battalion clerks in Leeds immediately dispatched 'Missing in action, believed killed' telegrams to the next of kin.

Not for a moment were the boys on the Somme expected to evade or defeat the advancing Germans, just slow them up long enough to allow the remainder of the Allies in northern France a bit of breathing space. Dunkirk is the story so often told, but, in truth, long after the 4th June, thousands more Allied troops were still in France, being shunted east, west and south as the game plan constantly changed. Eventually the fortunate survivors would be looking for their own escape routes.

Two weeks before, on the 31st May, Winston Churchill had ordered, in an atrocious French accent but nonetheless clearly, *"Partage bras-dessous!"* acting out an arm-in-arm gesture, that the BEF would evacuate with an equal number of other Allied troops. He went further, stating that the remaining British troops would form a rearguard as he would not accept further sacrifices by the French.

The platoon had no form of communications, no radio, not even a semaphore flag! This was commonplace for the majority of small units throughout northern France. Official records show the communications breakdown was worst in the west – an inevitable result of creating makeshift defence units. From the start of the war the French high command had rejected wireless. They believed that anyone could pick signals out of the air, and so placed all their faith in the telephone. This meant stringing miles and miles of cable and relying on overloaded civilian circuits, but at least the Boche wouldn't be listening. Not surprisingly, the advancing panzers chewed up some telephone lines, whilst Allied units moving here and there inadvertently cut other wires. Neither did it help when various headquarters regularly moved. General Gort's command post alone moved seven times in ten days. Exhausted signalmen could not string lines fast enough.

The new platoon of three sappers and their Highlander escort were to stand guard over their bridge at St Valery for about three days. Because the sappers had to be immediately on hand to blow the bridge, they found themselves having to live in an adjacent field. Here they constructed a temporary shelter out of straw, with only groundsheets supported by sticks to sleep on and another groundsheet to wrap around themselves. It was so uncomfortable that they were lucky to get any sleep, and clothing was permanently damp. Meanwhile, their infantry guards slept in some farm buildings a couple of hundred yards further away. Remarkably, the French farmer and his family were still living in the main farmhouse, but were to leave when the platoon did.

The infantrymen revealed that they had different orders once the bridge was demolished. Instead of following the river east as the Engineers had been ordered, they were to make their way west across country. After long discussion, the consensus opinion was that the river area would be hotly contested by the Germans, making it a dangerous escape route. The Cameronian captain was a man in his fifties, standing about five feet ten inches tall, smartly turned out even in combat fatigues. He had been a regular soldier before the war and was easily recognisable as what the Tommies would call a 'proper officer'. He sported a neatly trimmed military moustache and habitually carried a short silver-tipped swagger stick. He invited the three sappers, in his broad Scots accent, to accompany his platoon along their escape route, an offer which was gratefully accepted.

"Stand to," came the command from the captain, who was to prove himself time and again over the next few days to be cool under pressure. A no-nonsense man, he obviously knew just how to control his tough Highlanders. Issuing hastily prepared orders to his sergeant, he then turned to the three sappers and asked for a volunteer.

"One of you will have to stay behind to set the charges. Wait until you hear the adjacent bridge go up and, just as the Germans arrive, blow this bridge. Whoever does this will hopefully give the remainder of the Allied

Army precious time to retreat. The escort and I will wait for you at a safe distance. If that man is shot, one of the remaining two sappers will take his place. That's why there are three of you! Intelligence suggests that German forces, including panzer divisions, are rapidly gaining strength from the east. It is vital to slow their advance. It's up to us! We are the last defence."

Of course, what no one knew, because normal chains of command and control had broken down, was that the Germans had found a route through the 'impenetrable' Ardennes Forest far to the south and simply bypassed the Maginot Line. The 15th, 16th, 19th and 41st Panzer Corps had now swept into Belgium and northern France, wreaking havoc among defenders, bursting through the defensive lines, creating confusion and smashing supply lines, driving all before them. Within days yet more German tanks were at the Channel coast between Abbeville and Calais. But they paused, as Hitler wished to conserve his elite troops for the invasion of Paris. This was the stroke of luck that gave the BEF valuable time to install a somewhat fragile defensive line around Dunkirk, behind which the daring but vital evacuation had been staged.

One of you will have to stay behind to set the charges

18

By the 24th May the Allies were surrounded in a pocket based on Dunkirk, and the Germans had already advanced to both sides of the River Somme. It was not going to be 1914 all over again, despite 'red band' logic!

What was the first lesson every serviceman learnt? Oh yes – never volunteer! So why did Gil step forward that day? At six foot three and fit as a butcher's dog – apart from his rapidly deteriorating feet, that is – Gil was probably the ideal choice. His motto, which still endures to this day – 'If in doubt, punch it!' – was just what was needed at that moment. In truth, the other two sappers were already starting to make embarrassing excuses: iron lung, wooden leg, and a whole list of ailments and deformities no one had noticed before. One of them, a man Gil had no interest in getting to know, was a jailbird, given the option of military service or prison for some unknown villainy. Whatever, everyone just wanted to make for safe ground, but something within Gil stopped him. A sense of duty? He still cannot answer that one. Perhaps the officer had been a salesman before the war. If so, he must have been a damn good one because he convinced Gil that everything depended on him and he was the only man who could do it.

So what was this simple task again? Oh yes, stay behind as everyone else ran away; either wait for the sound of the adjacent bridge going up, or the Germans to appear on the opposite bank of the river (preferably both); move out into open ground, most likely under close fire; strike a match and light the fuses; then retreat to a safe distance and take cover – piece of cake!

For days, wherever Gil was, he had watched proud regiments of the BEF hurriedly evacuating the front line, which inexorably changed shape as it was pushed further back from all directions. Feelings of hopelessness were difficult to keep out of his mind. Surely the Allies could put up a better fight than this – all these brave men running for their lives! At least the Guards were marching in smart formation, rifles at the slope.

Disaster loomed. Back home the nation was in shock as the first Allied troops landed on the south coast of England, with graphic accounts of the desperate battles and rearguard actions raging a few short miles away in France.

"Where is the RAF?" – an angry question repeated by thousands of stranded Allied troops. Those wearing air-force-blue uniforms and still in France, unfairly bore the brunt of Army anger. Officially the RAF did fly a small number of sorties, but were moving squadrons closer to the

Channel in preparation for the forthcoming defence of Britain, so full-time cover could not be provided. None of this was known, or of help to Gil at that precise time. When it's you on the receiving end feelings endure. He still refers to it as 'a bloody disgrace'.

Meanwhile the Luftwaffe took full advantage. With so little opposition in the air, their only real problem was keeping up with the advancing panzers. Frequently taking off on missions and having to land at a new forward base, meant that their technical logistics, ground crews, fuel supplies, etc. had to be one step ahead. At the expense of the Allies they made the most of this short period, and referred to it as their 'golden days'!

Chapter III

"Staff car approaching, sir."

Gil's announcement brought a puzzled look from the captain, who was just about to leave with the rest of the platoon. The BEF car, with its front wing pendant fluttering manically in the breeze, roared up to the bridge and out leapt the CRE (commanding officer RE). He returned the captain's salute and, after a short exchange of greeting, proceeded to walk stiffly back and forth across the bridge as if impatiently tempting the German onslaught.

What made this totally bizarre for Gil and difficult not to laugh at was the cowboy-style low-slung revolver holster dangling on the right leg of the 'red band'. The sobering aspect was his right hand, which constantly hovered over the holster, like an itchy trigger finger at the OK Corral.

Moving uncomfortably close to Gil, who had remained at attention, the 'red band' looked straight into his eyes and with a curt, clipped military order said, "When you see a German tank on the bridge, blow it up, Sapper." Tension in the air was palpable.

"Yes, sir," was the crisp reply, but Gil considered this cowboy to be just as dangerous as any German; so relief was felt all around when, after these few surreal seconds, the CRE jumped back into his car and the pendant resumed its manic fluttering as his driver whisked him off toward the next bridge.

Hardly a morale boosting visit! But, despite everything, Gil gave this chap some credit for at least putting in an appearance at the eleventh hour.

Gil watched as the captain led the platoon and his fellow sappers away to safer ground. About two fields away, toward the farm, there they would wait for the reluctant hero to catch up with them. Time passed. He kept himself busy. Searching around the immediate area he located discarded munitions. Not wanting to make them a present to the Germans, he took it upon himself to place these extra items on his bridge, and so it was that an additional four tins of amatol explosive, and two large wooden cases, containing a total of thirty anti-tank mines, were carefully placed in the middle of an already well-charged bridge. He also donned two bandoliers across his chest, containing a total of 200 rounds of .303 ammunition. 'That should do it,' he thought and waited nervously for what seemed an eternity. Suddenly, from the direction of the next bridge, a distance of about two miles, he heard the unmistakable Wumph! as explosives were detonated.

That was the signal he had waited for – time to light and run. Of course, he could do the sporting thing and wait for the Germans to use him for target practice? Giving the two options careful consideration for at least half a millisecond, quite understandably he chose the former option. Stepping out from behind cover he crossed the open ground to the bridge, half expecting to hear the sound of small-arms fire and bullets whizzing past him. The bridge was clear, and there was no obvious sign of Allied comrades or civilians approaching on the far side. With his heart in his mouth he lit the one-and-a-half-minute fuses. So far so good. Then, without looking back, he turned and ran as fast as his suffering feet would permit. After the quickest 250-yard dash of his life, he came to a substantial-looking farm building. His masonry skills told him the solid stone pillars and lintel, which formed the ancient doorway, were the strongest features, so that was where he stood. Never was a theory so quickly proven.

At that relatively short distance, given the amount of official explosive and extra ordnance he had generously donated, the detonation was deafening. The ground momentarily turned to jelly and the shockwave was like a hammer blow. A split second later a loud crashing noise announced the earthbound arrival of several tons of concrete. Thrown up into the air and hurled hundreds of feet, it landed on his farm building. The roof collapsed and the walls seemed to implode. The only feature left standing was Gil's doorway. Most people would have entered that building! Saved again! 'A job well done,' thought he. They probably hadn't needed to blow the next bridge – if half as much debris fell there as had fallen here it was probably knocked down. With a bit of luck the Germans might have a flat tank or two as well!

The only feature left standing was Gil's doorway

The cross-country trek started for real, with the majority still in possession of full kit

Covered in dust, stunned by the explosion and the enormity of his lucky escape, he gathered his wits about him and continued to run through the fields. Not knowing exactly which direction to go, a sort of sixth sense guided him back to the platoon who by then were more than just the two fields away as first promised. They thought he was a goner, so had moved further back. "I wouldn't mind betting folks in the Highlands heard that bugger go up," was the politest remark made.

A quick "Well done. No time to lose, the Germans may be a tad annoyed by this, so best not wait for them!" said the captain and they were off.

Never slow off the mark, and with no RAF to contend with, the Luftwaffe soon appeared, sweeping up and down the river, strafing anything and everything with murderous machine-gun and cannon fire, just as the captain had predicted. By now the platoon had managed to reach the relative safety of an orchard, about a mile from the river, providing cover from marauding aircraft. There the pals spent a few brief moments to catch their breath and reflect on the task at hand. As they were to discover later, hundreds of bridges throughout northern France and the Belgian border had been demolished and inevitably many BEF troops had paid with their lives.

Respite over, the cross-country trek started for real, with the majority still in possession of full kit, naturally being reluctant to discard anything in case it should be needed. After a short distance all that was about to change. German patrols were everywhere, scouting for and ambushing stragglers like them, most likely intent on punishing someone for the destruction of the bridges.

Although the pals didn't know it at that time, reports were already being made of Allied prisoners of war being herded into buildings and yards where the SS blew them to pieces with stick grenades or mowed them down with machine guns. As an extra touch, some were executed by impromptu firing squads. Those obviously still alive were finished off with pistol and bayonet. Ninety-nine men of the 2nd Royal Norfolks at Locon paid this terrible price at the hands of the SS Totenkopf Division. Another tragic example saw eighty men of the 2nd Royal Warwicks forced to surrender after a hard-fought battle defending Wormhoudt. They were murdered by the SS Leibstandarte Adolf Hitler Regiment. The Second World War was to be littered with countless violations of basic human rights.

Amazingly, some men survived these wicked acts, hidden amid the bodies of their dead comrades. They later bore witness, exposing this evil to the world. Whereas those captured by the regular German Army, the Wehrmacht, were usually more fortunate. Their war was over, but at least they were alive and treated as fellow combatants.

The meandering course of the River Somme meant that the pals inevitably arrived back on its banks again. With their captain skilfully leading the platoon across open country, they now found themselves sidling along a building line. Suddenly, on reaching the corner of a bungalow, they were ambushed. The captain came face-to-face with a German wearing the unmistakable black uniform with death's head insignia of the SS, and a few short yards away were two stationary panzer tanks.

They were so close, having almost bumped into one another. The German was first to react. With the speed of a Wild West gunslinger, drawing his pistol, he stuck the muzzle into the captain's stomach and ordered all of them to surrender. The shock was total. You could always rely on someone's coarse barrack-room humour to give a glib response, but nobody said a word. You could cut the silence with a knife.

Suddenly there was a loud bang.

"What the hell was that?"

Everyone ducked, including the SS trooper. One of the lads behind Gil, purely through nervous fright, had squeezed the trigger of his rifle sending a .303 round aimlessly up into the air. For a few precious seconds confusion reigned, but this time the Tommies were first to react. "To the river!" shouted the captain. They didn't need much encouragement.

Gil, however, had instinctively dropped to a prone position and put a round into the breach. He took aim and, as the SS trooper scrambled to his feet, the German instantly dived for cover yet again. Frustratingly Gil never did get the chance to open fire – the German was too slippery a customer.

However, the confusion gave the captain and the rest of the platoon precious time to escape, but the German was not giving up that easily. He fired at least one shot, which thankfully missed the captain, but then passed within a fraction of an inch of Gil's ear. It was a unique sound he would never forget. However, it missed and, angry as he was, this was no time to introduce the German to a haymaker!

Not waiting around to discuss the etiquette of strategy and tactics, and thanks to the negligent discharge delaying any immediate organised German retaliation, the pals ran like hell. Gil managed to jump clear over a five-barred gate.

Continuing on for whatever protection the River Somme had to offer and, without hesitation, they all jumped into the water, hardly noticing how cold or deep it was and crouched behind whatever cover the embankment would afford. Gil found himself up to his chest in water, holding his rifle and ammunition bandoliers over his head. Sixty years on he still has a poignant reminder – the water-stained Army pay book he was carrying in the breast pocket of his tunic.

The SS trooper, now with the support of his comrades, was in hot pursuit, and with ruthless efficiency the tanks moved up and the Germans laid down a murderous barrage of machine-gun crossfire. Bullets were hitting the water just six feet out from the crouching Tommies, and slamming into the riverbank inches above their heads. There was no chance of firing a shot in defence as they were pinned down with no obvious escape route. One saving grace was that being so close the trajectory was too low for the tanks to bring their large gun barrels to bear, as was proven when a 75mm shell whistled harmlessly over their heads. Otherwise that would have been it.

Thoughts of being taken prisoner – or, worse, being killed in action with no one to say where or how they had bought it – were difficult to ignore. The only casualty was a sergeant who had crawled over the top of

Gil managed to jump clear over a five-barred gate

the riverbank to assess the situation and caught a bullet in his backside. Fortunately it was only a slight flesh wound. "Bit of a bummer, Sarge," muttered a cheeky Scots voice.

"Quickly now, put anything into the water that will float, like groundsheets, gas capes, anything!" The captain's voice was calm and measured. Within seconds the first items started to drift out into view of the Germans. Thinking about what he would have to carry and its useless design, Gil carefully placed selected items, including his tin hat, into the water and with a gentle push sent the big soup bowl on its final mission.

Would it work? The merciless hail of bullets continued for probably seconds, although it felt like minutes. Then, silence – the shooting had stopped. Had it worked? Did the Germans think the Tommies were goners? The captain, reliable as ever, didn't hesitate and quietly passed the word to follow him. Yet again luck was to smile on the platoon as they stealthily waded and crawled their way out of a seemingly hopeless position. Using the cover of thick reeds and bushes they managed to escape about half a mile upriver.

With no obvious indication the Germans had rumbled their ingeniously effective but no less daring feat of escapology, the platoon discovered a shallow point in the river, and out of sight of prying eyes they safely waded across in an orderly line. Still together, no one lost,

Gil wades across the River Somme

and the sergeant's wound causing no obvious problems. So far so good. It then dawned on Gil that his usual feelings of anger and a desire to punch someone's lights out must have been subconsciously put on hold. The moment had been too terrifying. Any gestures of insane defiance would have proved suicidal, but he has made up for it over the years!

The objective now was to make for the River Seine, a distance of about 110 miles. The platoon was split, forming two squads. The plan was to keep about eighty yards apart during daylight hours, then join up at night so as not to lose anyone in the darkness. After a few brief moments to get their breath back, and with darkness rapidly closing in, they set off again. Any thoughts of tiredness were soon dismissed, knowing the potential fate that awaited should the Germans find them. Remaining on a cross-country route, avoiding roads as much as possible, the two squads merged as one when darkness finally fell.

Apart from one all-too-brief stop in yet another orchard, they continued to walk on through the night, pausing only momentarily here and there so the captain could consult his map and compass. They covered many precious miles. On numerous occasions the night sky was turned into daylight, illuminated by a bright eerie glow, as the Germans sent up Very lights. Dangling on their tiny parachutes, these intense lights appeared from all directions, leaving the pals in no doubt that they were totally surrounded and being hunted.

All appeared still. The air was electric and silence was the strict order, as all too frequently the Germans were within feet of them – sometimes in the next field, but more often than not with only the darkness to hide their presence. One slight sound was all it needed to be discovered, and, at night, the Germans, who were most likely as jumpy as anyone else, would probably have shot first and asked questions later. It took nerves of steel to hold firm, but what a good job human nerves are not actually made of metal, because the way Gil's were jangling the whole of France would have heard them!

What a day! How could so many experiences be crammed into such a short time frame? Normality seemed a long way off as they continued their dogged walk toward the River Seine, but every man there had something to go back to – wife, family, home, or just a pint or two of ale. Whatever! – it was worth fighting for.

Chapter IV

Daybreak on day two of the platoon's retreat heralded the luxury of a fifteen-minute rest. Despite all he had been through, only now did Gil begin to think seriously about the state of his feet. Those Army doctors should never have passed him A1. Their comments at both medicals made it obvious they knew his feet were going to deteriorate rapidly. In fairness they could not have known the punishment about to be unleashed on them, and the extraordinary demands they would have to meet. Trade work, supervised by constant medical examination is one thing; front-line combat was not envisaged by anyone. Nevertheless, needs must at a time like that and this soldier was not about to quit. There would be plenty of time to sort it out later; right now he needed to be away on his toes – literally.

Keeping the eighty-yard rule, the two halves of the platoon plodded on through that day, only stopping for short breaks at irregular intervals, or to avoid detection by passing enemy patrols, including the Luftwaffe. Considering the number of German troops now flooding into that part of France, surrounding the Allies, it was a bold venture to say the least. In the meantime the remnants of battered battalions attempted to disrupt the German advance west toward Brittany, giving their beleaguered colleagues precious time to evacuate to Blighty.

The captain must have been tired – everyone else was – but he didn't make it too obvious as he continued to lead his platoon through the fields and along hedgerows, organising tasks, keeping people alert to the danger that was all around, then reacting skilfully to avoid capture. His map and compass were in constant use as he checked and rechecked the route. A lot of faith, trust and responsibility were being placed on his shoulders. He must have been working to some sort of strategic plan, but whether it was just his logic and reasoning, or general orders issued prior to chaperoning the sappers is not known. As their journey was to progress he gave the impression some of this was organised chaos, working to an agenda.

Long grass! Gil kept asking himself, 'Do French farmers cut grass for silage?' Because back home what they were walking through would have been collected in by now. Must be the labour shortage. Whatever, the grass was overdue for harvesting and whilst it provided good cover from ground level when they hit the dirt, the Luftwaffe pilots, roaming the skies unopposed must have seen the grass was trodden down, with tracks like big arrows pointing at the pals, saying, 'Shoot along the dotted line'! Numerous times enemy planes buzzed fields where they were, or where they had been walking, and the pals took whatever cover they could. Every time they expected a shower of hot metal to hit them, but their luck held up. Leaflets fluttered down all along the front, urging the Tommies to give up. Along with a crude map was a polite request in two languages, first to the French then to the BEF. It read:

British Soldiers!
Look at this map: it gives your true situation!
Your troops are entirely surrounded – stop fighting!
Put down your arms!

The addressees were most grateful, for without any form of direct communication it gave them a basic picture of the drama that had been Dunkirk and their reason for travelling west, tying up German resources, became crystal clear. Rather than becoming disheartened, it put the fight back into them. Of equal importance, the leaflets' strength and absorbency made good toilet paper!

The platoon struggled on all that day and again throughout the night. One of the other sappers was finding the going just a little too tough. Gil thought him a weakling as this chap continually moaned and said he wanted to sit down and give up. But, without hesitation, private thoughts put aside, Gil took hold of him and surprisingly enough the jailbird sapper did the same, so between them they supported their colleague for many miles, across more ploughed fields, along a railway line, over barbed-wire fences and hedges, through ditches, occasionally waist-deep in water, but despite everything they made excellent progress and valuable miles were covered.

They lived off a meagre diet of hard-tack biscuits that a dog would turn its nose up at and precious water. Of course the jailbird sapper may well have called that a square meal. Gil thought better than to ask, preferring to keep his own counsel and save the fight for the Germans if it came to that.

Each night proved to be a carbon copy of the previous one. The Germans and the Tommies knew the other was out there, somewhere, but thankfully the platoon remained undiscovered despite many a close encounter as they plodded on.

Chapter V

Day three saw another all too brief rest at sunrise. The previous night had taken its punishing toll, sapping precious strength, but the cliché is quite true, 'When the going gets tough, the tough get going' and this band of brothers were just as determined to press on. They were buoyed up by their enormous good fortune to date, the distance covered and faith in the captain. By his reckoning, the platoon could maintain their present rate of progress, which, allowing for rest breaks, had averaged out at just under three miles per hour.

Over the total time span, which, including the distance yet to be covered, was about thirty-eight hours, the captain anticipated they would reach the River Seine by the afternoon of that day. There, with more good fortune, they could meet up with other members of the rearguard and have strength in numbers.

Give a man hope, an objective that by all common reasoning appears achievable, put that in a theatre of war, when he also knows a ruthless enemy is actively hunting for him and if caught may treat him as a fifth columnist and shoot him on sight, as opposed to being seen as a fellow soldier and afforded the courtesy of prisoner-of-war status – the desire to press on becomes a potent incentive.

The captain's calculations were proven to be spot-on. The platoon reached the banks of the River Seine at about midday. Being seasoned campaigners by now in the art of escape and evasion, they instinctively made good use of the natural cover provided by bushes, undergrowth and reeds along the riverbank. They did not have to wait long. Whilst peering through a thick bed of reeds Gil saw two men in civilian clothing on the opposite bank. With no time to debate the possibility of them being hostile, and because of the pressing need to cross the river, which

33

looked pretty wide and deep, the captain took a calculated risk and started waving to attract their attention.

"Do you think they understand semaphore?" someone asked.

"Why, does anyone here know semaphore?" enquired the captain.

The silence and shaking heads confirmed the stupidity of the question. In any event, the odds in favour of these two individuals having served as flag-waving signallers in the French military were longer than Hitler winning the Nobel Peace Prize!

After much hand-waving, the two civilians eventually saw the semi-hidden platoon and waved back.

"They look friendly enough. Let's see if a simple gesticulation of the arm, like a policeman waving on the traffic will work," suggested the captain.

Judging by the activity on the far bank, that simple signal was also used by the gendarmes at French road junctions, because the two civilians were soon busy propelling a rowing boat directly toward the waiting platoon.

The tension was palpable. Then a broad Scots accent cut through the air: "Och! You're a dark horse, sir. You never let on you could speak Frog!" Cheeky Cameronian humour was usually a welcome diversion during these all too frequent situations and the captain was amused!

As soon as their new Gallic friends arrived it was immediately obvious the boat could only carry five passengers at a time. Gil was in the third group and, after a total of nine trips, everyone had been ferried safely across. The captain practised his signalling skills again and after much vigorous handshaking, accompanied by a few nods, a pat on the back or two, and a cheesy grin, the French language was mastered, and their grateful thanks was conveyed to the two gallant rowers. Even the jailbird sapper showed his appreciation by not picking their pockets!

After a brief pause to check the map, take a compass bearing, and enquire after everybody's general condition, they were off on the next stage of the adventure. Having walked only a few yards, another lifesaving stroke of luck befell them: they met up with BEF 'line of communication' troops – odds and sods, in other words – who had made their way from Rouen. The best bit was that they had about fifteen lorries hidden in woods near the river. Hurrah! – the first real chance for our heroes to give their feet a well-deserved rest.

Probably not to be found in any Second World War reference book, or Army war diary, was the impromptu formation of a brand-new 'temporary' regiment. On meeting up with the other units the old pals were introduced to a rifle-regiment officer, a larger-than-life, charismatic individual called Captain Newcome. He took it upon himself, presumably with the blessing of his brother officers, to take a roll-call and interview each man in turn to establish his original unit, his skills and health status. Such was the dynamic effect on morale that the odds and sods, who by now represented numerous regiments and corps, started to affectionately refer to themselves collectively as Newcome's Rifles. The name stuck, and, even when other stragglers joined in along the way, they were quick to adopt the new unofficial regimental name.

This new band of brothers was, quite simply, in need of mutual support and good leadership. In Newcome's Rifles they found all that. From the exchange of information, it soon became apparent that they had all been deliberately left behind not only to cover a retreat, but to tie down numerous German divisions, allowing the evacuation of hundreds of thousands of other Allied troops from north-western France and perhaps giving the French divisions guarding Paris half a fighting chance.

The diversity of experiences and stories being told was vast. Inevitably, as with any epic drama, there were tales to amuse and horrify, elate and sadden. Some had fought desperate hand-to-hand battles, whilst other lucky individuals had seen neither hide nor hair of a German. Whatever – job done, now it was their turn to beat a retreat.

For the first time in five days the St Valery platoon were dry. How no one went down with a serious ailment is a mystery, as they had been constantly wet, sleeping in the open, or in deserted farmhouses. As they trudged along it had rained all that previous night into the next day. Gil slept well, tucked up in one of the lorries hidden in the woods, close to the point where the old platoon had been boating on the Seine earlier that day.

On the Home Front bad news was being delivered. Gil's parents received the official telegram, generated in Leeds, but purportedly from the War Office, notifying them that their son was 'Missing in action, believed killed.' Not approving of their son's friendship with Beryl, they deliberately kept the news from her for a couple of days. Eventually they did condescend to tell her, but only then after she went to Braunton to confront them – the news was understandably heartbreaking.

In typical Beryl fashion she swiftly recovered and steadfastly refused to believe the message in the telegram, so two days later when the Field Service Post Card sent by Gil back at Forges-les-Eaux arrived, she took it to a local fortune-teller, one Alice Saunders, a crystal ball amateur from Barnstaple, who held it and promptly announced that she could see three men walking along a railway line. One was being carried, but Gilbert was all right. This was proof enough for Beryl. Bolstered by her own intuition she firmly believed that Gil was alive. Strange but true – as previously mentioned, that is exactly what had occurred in France.

Gil's Field Service Post Card

NOTHING is to be written on this side except the date and signature of the sender. Sentences not required may be erased. If anything else is added the post card will be destroyed.

[Postage must be prepaid on any letter or post card addressed to the sender of this card.]

I am quite well.

~~I have been admitted into hospital~~

{ sick and am going on well.

{ ~~wounded and hope to be discharged soon.~~

~~I am being sent down to the base.~~

I have received your { letter dated ___

{ telegram „ ___

{ parcel „ ___

Letter follows at first opportunity.

I have received no letter from you

{ lately

{ for a long time.

Signature only } *Sapper G Mack*

Date *June 12th*

Forms /A2042/7. 51-4997.

37

Chapter VI

On day four, Newcome's Rifles awoke at first light to the awesome sight and sounds of the German Army moving troop carriers, tanks and artillery along the opposite bank of the River Seine, within full view of yesterday's makeshift ferry route. This seemingly endless military tide was flowing in the direction of Rouen. If they were aware of the Tommies' presence, they wasted no time on them. In any event the bridges had been blown and the ferry had vanished. German sights at that time were set on securing the territory so rapidly gained, and consolidating their power base before the push toward Paris.

The briefing was short and simple: Le Mans was their next objective and the lorries formed an orderly convoy for the journey south. What bliss to renew their acquaintance with that much-loved medieval-style torture known as the Army lorry, an important source of income for a chiropractor! But these were extraordinary circumstances.

With the German Army still on their tail and all that footslogging cross-country punishment recently endured, this time it was put up and shut up. This ride was a true luxury. The lorry Gil adopted was well stocked with hard-tack ration tins, not quite Fortnum & Mason quality, but never look a gift horse and all that! The most interesting item to be found in each tin was a four-inch-square by one-inch-thick bar of chocolate, which allegedly contained a nutritious blend of different ingredients that should be eaten slowly, in small doses. They had been warned about consuming it too ravenously! Gil never did discover what they were packed with – probably bromide!

Throughout the 180-mile journey, tired eyes kept constant vigil. Surely the Luftwaffe were bound to find them sooner or later? But Lady Luck continued to smile and nothing was seen of the enemy. As a result, the convoy did stop for a brief coffee break at a small café at Alençon, in Normandy, where Gil managed to find a stale crust of bread, but the respite was shattered by a French civilian who burst in, waving his arms about, gibbering and obviously well agitated. Fortunately one of the Tommies understood enough French to decipher the hysterical message. A rough translation: "Bugger off, the Germans are only five kilometres down the road, coming in this direction." No prizes for guessing the next move!

Something the convoy could not have known was that coastal weather conditions had turned sour, with steady drizzle and a ceiling of only 300 feet, so the Luftwaffe remained on the ground. The local commanding officer, Major General Wolfram von Richthofen, a distant cousin of the famous Red Baron, had the added frustration of briefing his Gruppe leaders that, by agreement with Army Group B, only the beaches and shipping would be attacked. There were no targets inland for fear of hitting their own troops. That afternoon the weather cleared!

Some eight hours later Gil arrived at Le Mans safe and sound. Yet more lorries and troops joined the convoy. There was no time to pass pleasantries or exchange stories – just a quick refuel, a change of driver and off again. This time the objective was Rennes, about 140 miles west. For the second time, the convoy enjoyed an unopposed journey. "Perhaps the Germans enjoyed their days on the beach and have buggered off back home," suggested one optimistic Tommy!

Just short of six weary hours due west via Laval and the first vehicle in the convoy entered Rennes and, of course, there to meet them were yet more lorries. The convoy grew to about 100 vehicles and approximately 2,000 men. The opportunity to meet and talk with others was irresistible and it soon became obvious they had all played small but crucial parts in a grand theatre of rearguard action, deliberately tasked with holding back the German Army for as long as possible, and giving the main bulk of the BEF a chance to reach home shores.

Some units, with orders to dig in, had literally fought to the last man. So the convoy had been planned after all, including the rendezvous at Le Mans and Rennes. Gil could not thank the captain of Cameron Highlanders enough. Had it not been for his map-reading skills and leadership immediately following the St Valery bridge demolition, they would not have found the convoy, even if luck had played a part back at Rouen.

Based on intelligence gathered from the vast array of different units now represented in the convoy (predominantly Scottish regiments),

Captain Newcome would have most likely considered the Germans had delayed their push west in order to mop up Dunkirk and prevent the Allies forming a permanent beachhead. After that they would have turned their elite units south, for what Hitler must have seen as the real prize, Paris. Convinced by this theory, which was later proven correct, coupled with their miraculous 300-mile, almost trouble-free drive all the way from Rouen, Newcome decided to ride this good luck and ordered the entire convoy to park up for the night on the St Malo road, just outside Rennes.

With endless tales of daring deeds circulating around the lorries, it was soon apparent this rapidly expanding temporary regiment of odds and sods had all suffered varying degrees of danger and hardship. So, that night, as a special treat, they wined and dined yet again on Adam's ale and those much loved Army-issue hard-tack rations, which had a clearly printed use-by date of July 1916. The biscuits were so reminiscent of mini paving slabs that many a good tooth, including Gil's dentures were cracked on them, but at least his feet had been given a rest.

One factor had, however, surprised them throughout the journey, and that was the small number of civilian refugees moving west. There were some discarded belongings, abandoned carts and vehicles, and people walking alongside the road, but not so many as to become a hindrance to their convoy. The majority of the highways were clear.

Chapter VII

Gil and the rest of the original platoon had slept so well in the back of their lorry, that when they awoke on the morning of day five and stuck their heads out through the canvas flap, their puzzled faces must have made a comical sight whilst trying to decide if this was a bad dream or reality. The road was deserted, and there was only one vehicle left – theirs. Jumping down from the back, they found their driver still snoring away in the cab, oblivious to the drama outside, but once roused he quickly breakfasted on a mouthful of ripe obscenities, interspaced with the unmentionable things he would do to the others if he ever found them again!

The lorry soon picked up speed toward St Malo, on what they all prayed was the final 70-or-so-mile journey through France. But the pals were angry: Why didn't someone wake them? What if the Germans had found them? Why had the convoy deserted them? Surely someone could have checked rather than just drive past them? There were plenty of questions, but no answers.

As the final leg of 'Newcome's Luxury Tours' trundled on toward the seaside, anger gradually turned to reasoning and the most favoured conclusion as to why the convoy left them behind was that those parked behind them, confused and half asleep, thought the lorry had broken down and then made the classic erroneous assumption that someone else had physically checked inside the vehicle! This thought cheered them up for all of five minutes, before new conspiracy theories came to mind and, from comments made, murderous thoughts were obviously contemplated by one or two less forgiving types.

About three hours later they reached the outskirts of St Malo where they joined a queue of lorries approaching the old walled city and, as the

41

docks loomed into view, there, in the outer harbour, were two boats – a destroyer and a steamer. What a sight!

"This is it, the ticket home, boys."

It mattered not who said it, these were magical words that forgave all but a few previous transgressions.

Soon after arrival, an officer in charge of marshalling troop movements at the docks ordered them to hand over the faithful lorry that had safely carried the pals for over 370 miles. It was unceremoniously dumped into the inner harbour, along with over a hundred other vehicles and assorted items of large equipment. The idea was to deny the Germans immediate access to all the port facilities. Some vehicles were pushed over the sea cliffs.

Gil and his pals were the last to arrive and the very last to leave St Malo on the last boat out. They made their way to the outer harbour where, assigned to a boat, Gil boarded the steamer. It was packed. The rest of Newcome's Rifles were already on board, and again the collective tension was tangible. Would their luck run out? Would the Luftwaffe find them? Would Gil deliver Captain Newcome a punch on the nose for leaving Rennes without them that morning? The truth is that Gil was so grateful for someone taking command and organising their retreat, including the leadership of their Cameron Highlander captain, that at that precise moment he would have forgiven anyone, except the Germans, just about anything.

Consensus opinion aboard ship was that St Malo must be considered a valuable prize by the Germans, perhaps as a launch point for the invasion of the Channel Islands and raids on targets along the English south and west coasts. So, in that case, not wanting to inflict too much structural damage on the port, they would wait for the two boats to leave harbour before attacking. Tension turned to a form of paranoia, as eyes again searched the sky for any sign of air attack, whilst the boats, crammed with their precious human cargo, waited motionless in port, like sitting ducks, longing for the cover of darkness before putting to sea.

Although Gil could not be described as a religious man, there was no doubt in his mind that someone's God must have been on their side those last few days. At that particular moment, as a helpless target on board ship, with nowhere to run and hide, his private prayers were answered. As the daylight hours slowly and nervously ticked away, not one air raid came in. Perhaps the Germans were too busy celebrating their triumphant entrance into Paris.

Official records state that 21,000 Allied troops were evacuated from St Malo between the 16th and 17th June. Here were our reluctant heroes almost one week later, yet there was no mention in dispatches for them. Remarkable order and discipline was maintained, probably because they were too weary to behave otherwise.

On Gil's steamer, however, one ravenous chap found a crate of corned beef and, without standing on ceremony, lifted it above his head and threw it onto the deck. The crate shattered and numerous tins were strewn around. Fortunately Gil was close by and managed to grab one before they all disappeared under a rugby scrum of desperately famished men. This was the first proper food he had eaten for several days. He was so hungry that he could have devoured the tin as well, but for the fact that his dentures had been broken on those Army hard-tack rations the night before.

It was blatantly obvious to most that Newcome's Rifles, which was entirely made up of BEF soldiers, must have been planned at some stage. At every major town or city along the way additional troops had been waiting for the convoy. The two ships at St Malo must also have been part of the grand scheme, sent especially for them, anticipating their arrival. Was there a remote possibility a 'red band' worked it all out? Again official records show that tens of thousands of Allied troops poured west and the lucky ones found ships awaiting their arrival at Le Havre, Cherbourg, St Malo, Brest and Vannes, and no doubt other escape routes were utilised. The only other member of his company sent to blow the Somme bridges, whom Gil can recall seeing within Newcome's Rifles, or indeed for several days yet to come, was the lad, Ansell, from South Molton, the one he joined up with, who was by now a lorry driver.

As darkness fell 'the last boat home' put to sea. It was some fourteen hours after boarding and the tension dared to ease a little. The 'cruise' back to home shores took all night. Apparently they had to be landed at Dover so the military authorities could officially count them all in! How ridiculous was that, sending them right into the danger zone, across the German guns now covering the Pas de Calais! Fears of a Luftwaffe or S-boat attack never materialised, and neither did the mess steward with a gin and tonic! Still, the weather was kind, providing a fairly smooth passage.

Once his fellow passengers had settled down, Gil was able to find some space to stretch his legs, but, search as he may, he just could not find the saloon bar! Over the next few hours the enormity of his lucky escape was to fill his thoughts. The tonic of good fortune was intoxicating enough.

Chapter VIII

The two boats travelled within sight of each other throughout the night, reaching Dover at daybreak. Just as they were passing the harbour wall about to enter the port, four Spitfires flew low overhead. They were the first RAF planes seen for weeks. One or two choice comments went skywards. Then, as now, if you fight a war, air cover is essential. You must control the skies.

But the Royal Air Force was soon to prove its mettle, displaying superhuman qualities of strength and courage. As the nation licked the wounds of Dunkirk, the Battle of Britain was about to start. With the Luftwaffe consolidating its position in Belgium and France through June and July, they tested British opposition with tentative strikes against various targets. On the 2nd August, Reich Marshal Hermann Goering issued the 'Eagle Day' directive – the destruction of the British air defences prior to a landing by German forces. It soon became clear, however, that this was going to be no easy victory for the Germans.

Although bombing raids against Britain's cities continued well into 1941, it was clear to all, even as early as the 15th September 1940 (the date Hitler had set aside for the first phase of Operation Sea Lion, the planned invasion of Britain), that without the ability to dominate the skies the operation was postponed. Germany formally abandoned the invasion plan on the 12th October.

The Battle of Britain was over and there was no disputing the fact that the British had won. Prime Minister Winston Churchill addressed parliament with his memorable statement, "Never in the field of human conflict was so much owed by so many to so few." On a much smaller scale, the heroic efforts of those left behind in France to cover the evacuation of the Allies could be compared.

Moments before the ship docked at Dover, Gil found the captain of Cameron Highlanders and thanked him from the bottom of his heart, for it was he who had saved the platoon. Had it not been for his expert map-reading and compass skills, together with his coolness under fire, most likely none of them would have been setting foot on English soil that day. Gil knew how lucky he had been. So many didn't make it! If only he could remember the captain's name!

When eventually the pals disembarked at Dover, there was no brass band to greet them, and no flag-waving crowd of well-wishers, but of course they had not been part of the main evacuation force. They were the rearguard, the 'fullbacks' left behind and reported missing or killed. They expected nothing, but those they did meet were hearty enough and made them feel welcome. The ordeal of recent days was mirrored in their unshaven faces, hollow eyes and infinite weariness. Hungry and pale, the emotion of setting foot on home soil was too difficult to hide, even for some of the real hard men.

After a short walk they arrived at a school where they spent the night under the ever watchful eye of an officer. His sole job it was to ensure they didn't eat too much because of the delicate state their stomachs were in. It took a couple of days for Gil to become used to proper food again.

Apart from a big grin, the pals must have looked a sorry state. All Gil had left was the dirty uniform he stood up in, his forage cap, rifle, bayonet and the two ammunition bandoliers. After a night's rest, these very last evacuees from France climbed aboard a train, which took them to an emergency tented Army camp near Stonehenge, Salisbury. They were told that this temporary camp, comprised of row after row of large bell tents, each containing ten men, would be home for a number of weeks. Well, after just nine days that came to an abrupt end when one chap, determined to go home, voiced his feelings by 'accidentally' dropping a cigarette which set his sleeping bag alight, thus destroying the bell tent and its entire contents. Fortunately nobody was hurt, but the ten occupants lost all their kit and equipment.

Prior to that last Field Service Post Card sent on the 12th June from France, Gil had regularly corresponded with Beryl by letter and she in turn sent messages of encouragement, together with those all-important supplies of tobacco. During these exchanges, the basic arrangements for their wedding were discussed and they had agreed that on his next home leave, whenever that was, they would be married.

There was no formal engagement, but the circumstances were so extraordinary that, as soon as the officer commanding the tented camp at Salisbury announced they would all be given a forty-eight-hour pass, Gil sent a telegram to Beryl on the 30th June, stating he was safe in England and would be home the next day on leave. Unbeknown to Gil, this was the first news of his safe return. Neither the Army, nor the War Office had bothered to notify the next of kin that their loved ones were alive!

Beryl acted immediately, booked her local church, St Mary Magdalene, in Bear Street, Barnstaple, for the following day and rallied help from friends and family. Beryl's father cycled the five miles to Braunton and broke the good news to Gil's parents – one can only imagine the emotion of that moment.

Armed with just a forty-eight-hour pass, Gil made his way home to North Devon. Time was a luxury and after some rapid last-minute organising, including having his dentures fixed (broken on those hard-tack rations back in France). Incredible as it may sound, he still uses those same dentures; sixty years later they're still going strong.

So, with not a minute to waste, having to forgo the usual formality of an engagement and stag party, he donned a civilian suit and married Beryl. But why marry during the turmoil and uncertainty of war? Their answer was quite simple: it seemed the right thing to do. They had no thoughts of the future, just of living for today.

Their wedding night was spent at Gil's parents' house in Braunton, but those precious hours passed rapidly and all too soon he found himself standing on Barnstaple Town Railway Station, awaiting yet another train to take him away from those he loved. Beryl was to return to her parents' house in Barnstaple, where she would remain for the duration of the war and beyond. Gil spent that night back in Salisbury, where he and the other engineers picked up their kit and prepared for the next adventure.

Chapter IX

Awaking in Salisbury, his orders took him by train to Leeds. There, at Roundhay Park, the men of the 670th Artesian Works Company, Royal Engineers, including all the veterans of France, were to meet again. By some miracle not one engineer had been lost. In stark contrast, however, they discovered that over half of the infantrymen assigned to escort the Somme pals had been captured or killed. The three Fates of mythology must have a soft spot for sappers!

Gil also learnt that he and the other two sappers in his bridge-blowing team were the only ones missing when the other 247 Somme heroes returned to England just a day or two after their demolition exercise was completed. Who knows what would have happened? What they did know was that the Germans were very active in their sector strafing the riverbanks, so perhaps they did make the right decision to stay with their infantry guard. Whatever, they were back.

The company were to spend the next four weeks being knocked back into shape, Army-style (parades, marching and routine drills)! No doubt this was happening at bases all over the British Isles as regiments, corps, squadrons, ships' companies and other units were reunited or reorganised, to restore some semblance of order into the armed services in preparation to defend home shores. For the Engineers, with so many troops in poor physical state after recent ordeals (including the terror of marriage!) it was a chance to build the men up again prior to their next important and labour-intensive task. Yorkshire people proved in the main to be very hospitable and many a pint of ale was 'forced' upon him. Well, it's rude to say no! However, their friendliness was comforting and much appreciated.

The second course of square-bashing and routine Army fatigues completed, the company gained a few new faces and lost some originals, including all the other North Devon pals he had joined with, who were assigned to different companies. Meanwhile, Gil remained with the 670th and was posted to Cornwall.

Their long train journey south was interrupted by an overnight stop in Plymouth, a city that was to suffer horrendous bombing raids, as the Germans pounded the historic Devonport Naval Base. Of vast strategic importance to the nation since 1691, it was a prime target for the Luftwaffe. Fortunately, choosing a quiet night, the company slept on the floor of a dance hall.

Next morning they entrained to continue their journey west. Optimistically, many pals had packed a bucket and spade, but were soon to realise this was not going to be a traditional seaside holiday. Far from it! The next twelve months turned into a non-stop chain of building projects, fortifying English Channel coastal defences.

After all the destruction witnessed in France, Gil was looking forward to this period of construction. Apart from the stunning scenery along the Cornish coast, this is just what he thought he had joined to do – build things. Perhaps now he would receive that extra trade pay as promised when he signed up back in the recruiting office in Barnstaple. To date he and the other skilled sappers had only been paid half that amount and, blunted by their experiences in France, feelings of injustice ran high within the ranks.

As trains pull out of Plymouth the track leaves the county of Devon, crossing the River Tamar, over the Prince Albert Railway Bridge, built by that most famous of Victorian engineers, Isambard Kingdom Brunel in 1859. On the opposite bank the train entered Saltash and the county of Cornwall. Its rich diverse heritage included the legendary seat of King Arthur, a unique but seldom used Brythonic Celtic language, the Ancient Order of Druids who survive to this day and a Stannary Parliament which once presided over countless 19th-century tin and copper mines (all now closed), together with a wealth of fascinating towns and villages, making it one of the most popular British holiday destinations.

Helston Railway Station was the company jumping-off point. Stepping down onto the platform, they gathered their kit and climbed aboard those infamous Army lorries for the last stage of the journey to the picturesque, peacetime fishing village of Porthleven. There they constructed a camp, starting as always with their own living accommodation, progressing to the canteen, stores and other essential buildings that no self-respecting Army camp could do without. Company Headquarters based themselves

The Fowey team – Gil, back row without his forage cap

in the small cathedral city of Truro, from where, over the next twelve months, the commanding officer and his staff would direct working parties of various sizes to defence projects all along the south coast of Cornwall.

A few days later, Gil was placed in an eight-man working party, issued with a lorry and led by a Lance Corporal Hughes. These lucky pals were privileged enough to be sent into lodgings, for about four weeks, in the beautiful hillside village of Fowey. With narrow streets that twist steeply down to a small quay, in peacetime ships laden with china clay from St Austell mingle with pleasure craft. Not that anyone was doing much leisure sailing at that time, for fear of being blown out of the water by submerged mines or marauding Germans. Gil has a photograph of the work detail, taken outside their lodgings. Unfortunately, due to the passage of time, he can only name Lance Corporal Hughes.

Such was the fear of German invasion, that every conceivable landing place, especially on that south coast, was identified and fortified as best possible. At Fowey, standing adjacent to the harbour wall was a lodging house for mariners, not surprisingly named the Sailor's Rest – their temporary barracks. In the back garden the pals built a concrete pillbox, from which machine guns had a commanding arc of fire across the harbour – a construction pattern followed at countless sites.

On a number of occasions the Germans launched night-time bombing raids on Plymouth city centre and Devonport Naval Base. Even though the pals were approximately twenty miles away, the roar of high explosives detonating caused the ground to shake like jelly, along with everything else; items on shelves would fall to the floor – a truly terrifying experience. Having never witnessed an earthquake, Gil imagined there must be similarities. The one pervading thought as he lay in relative safety amid the total blackout at Fowey, was for the poor brave souls in Plymouth on the receiving end of the Blitz. Of course, Gil could relate in part to his own spectacular 'firework display' at St Valery, when the bridge almost landed on his head. By stark contrast the populated city of Plymouth was being bombarded time and again by thousands of tons of high explosive – an awesome nightmare.

Gil and his team were to construct many octagonal pillboxes over the next year, along with miles of barbed-wire barricades and minefields planted across beaches from Polperro to Land's End. Unfortunately accidents were commonplace, with sappers stepping on or mishandling mines and blowing themselves up, or becoming entangled in razor-sharp wire, or falling whilst working on the edge of sheer cliff tops. There were any number of hazardous situations for which today's Health and Safety laws would provide a degree of protection for workers, by the use of specialist equipment or clothing, with the realistic chance of reasonable financial compensation. A momentary lapse of concentration was all it took to endanger yourself and anyone else in close proximity.

After a couple of months moving from job to job, the work details always returned to the main camp at Porthleven for reassignment. With home-leave entitlement being only once every three months and not having had a honeymoon, Beryl, being the determined character she was, and still is, decided to visit Gil instead. This was discouraged by the military, but it wasn't going to stop her! Arriving late because of a missed connection at Exeter when a platform porter gave her erroneous information, it was 10 p.m. before she eventually stepped onto the platform of Helston Railway Station, where Gil had been waiting patiently for several hours. Due to the time of day and the blackout, there were no buses running, so wearing totally impractical, but very smart, high-heeled shoes, she handed her suitcase to Gil and the two of them walked the three miles to a small hotel in Porthleven, where she had pre-booked a room. Also lodging there were some Army officers. Gil was permitted to visit her, but under strict orders to return to barracks each evening.

Having never been away from home before, Beryl discovered she was afraid to be alone; neither did it help with the hotel being so close to the harbour mouth. She could both see and hear waves crashing against the sea wall, and having never experienced this it all added to her feeling of unease. Consequently she hardly slept a wink. So the next day Gil made an earnest plea to the duty officer, who took pity and allowed him on compassionate grounds to stay with Beryl for the remainder of her visit, which was originally going to be one week. If this was a ruse, it worked! But a couple of the chinless-wonder-type officers staying at the hotel were decidedly uncomfortable with a private soldier in their 'mess'.

Some honeymoon! With Gil having to work every day, Beryl found herself on her own. The wife of Gil's commanding officer was apparently staying in the same hotel, although Beryl never saw her. The husband-and-wife team who owned and ran the premises were friendly enough, but there was only so much to do and see for this lively townee.

At night, even though Plymouth was about seventy miles away, they could hear the dull thud of explosions, and the night sky on the horizon was often lit by an eerie glow as German bombers pounded the city.

Meanwhile, with no daytime company and little to amuse her, Beryl soon became bored. After just three days she decided to return home to Barnstaple. Gil was given permission to escort her to Helston Railway Station, but this time they rode in a bus; Beryl's flimsy high-heeled shoes would not have survived another hike.

Just by way of a final irony to end the ill-fated 'honeymoon', as Beryl climbed into the railway carriage, Gil accidentally slammed the door on her thumb. Holding back the tears even though the pain was excruciating, she stoically maintained a degree of dignity. They said their farewells and she settled down for the journey with the other passengers. Some had seen what had happened and offered friendly words of comfort. Gil meanwhile returned to barracks.

That was to be the first and last time Beryl did anything quite so adventurous. From there on, for the remainder of his Army service, Gil was to receive two weeks' leave roughly once every three months, and he did the visiting.

One of the most important projects was at Porthcurno, just a couple of miles south of that most south-westerly point on the British mainland, Land's End. For this was the home of both the transatlantic telephone cable and a vitally important maritime and air-defence wireless station. Here, the shore defences had to be robust, with pillboxes providing a complete arc of fire across the beach, and a range of other obstacles to protect the seaward approaches to this vital lifeline with the United States of America. They also built small Nissen huts for the artillerymen who were permanently stationed there, together with purpose-built emplacements for their heavy guns.

Lodgings would move every so often to keep pace with their building progress. After three months at Porthleven the company moved to Falmouth, where they started building new billets for both themselves and again the local artillery detachment, who had ack-ack gun sites all over the area. This time they pitched camp within the 400-year-old fortifications of Pendennis Castle, at Falmouth. Built between 1539 and 1543, the castle sits on a lofty perch overlooking the English Channel entrance to the Carrick Roads waterway, where seven estuaries meet. Falmouth, a busy port since Tudor times, lays claim to have been the first mail-packet station, in 1688. Fast sailing ships took mail overseas from here for some 150 years.

Renowned by mariners throughout the world as a natural harbour, with excellent boatyard facilities, the Admiralty considered it of vital strategic importance. There is little doubt the SKL, German Naval War Command, thought the same, especially as the Royal Yacht *Britannia* was stationed there, serving as the floating base for a motor-torpedo-boat squadron. What a propaganda coup and blow to British morale that would have been if the Germans had sunk or captured *Britannia*.

Every morning, with nerves of steel, the MTB crews would race their boats at breathtaking speed in a V formation, out toward the English Channel in a deliberate noisy manoeuvre. Their wooden hulls were designed to minimise the danger from detonating magnetic mines which had either strayed or been dropped by the Germans into open waters. Relying on their speed to avoid disaster, they would then patrol the coastline both east and west looking for trouble.

Whilst taking in the natural beauty of Carrick Roads from the vantage point of his fort, Gil just happened to be watching a daily routine mine-trawling exercise one day, by a two-masted wooden-built vessel, when, instead of safely locating and repositioning mines, it hit one. The huge explosion sent a spout of water high into the air. The wooden hull stood no chance, and the vessel sank without trace within two minutes. Fortunately it had been towing a small dinghy into which the surviving crew were able to scramble.

On another day, Gil was working near Falmouth golf course, when he saw a dog run onto an adjacent inland antipersonnel minefield, little more than a few feet away from him. The unfortunate mutt was promptly blown to pieces, the debris being thrown up and over Gil's head, landing fifty yards behind him.

The 670th Artesian Works Company were retained on the Cornwall coastal defence project for another ten months, covering many miles of contrasting scenery, from soft sandy beach to boulder- and pebble-strewn shore, rising to the dramatic sheer cliff faces weathered by Atlantic storms as best seen on the Lizard Peninsula. Of course the weather played a major part in all this, with some of those infamous westerly gales lashing into the pals as they toiled to build those all-important defences. Every now and again they would receive gruesome reminders of the potential threat of invasion, when bodies, dressed in German uniforms, were washed up along the coast. There was little doubt that attempts to land were made by small raiding parties, but if any did succeed, it wasn't common knowledge.

Just as it had been during childhood, every now and again someone would push the wrong button and Gil would feel the need to deliver a haymaker. One such incident occurred at Polperro, just to the east of Fowey. On a cliff top, high above the beach, Gil was with another small team of eight sappers, led by a weedy little weasel of a lance corporal on secondment from HQ in Truro, where his onerous duties as a clerk usually kept him safe and dry! This chap was temporarily filling in whilst the regular NCOs were on a training course.

Their task at Polperro was to erect barbed-wire fencing along the cliff edge. It was heavy and potentially dangerous work if not done properly. The wire was wound around large wooden drums, each weighing several hundred pounds when full. The technique for carrying these drums was to place a handle through the middle, and at least two chaps would lift and walk. Lance Corporal Weasel had spinelessly allowed the malingering half of his platoon to visit a local farm to scrump apples. So, being short-handed, he ordered Gil, allegedly in an offensive and abrupt manner, to do all the heavy lifting expected of the full platoon. Quite naturally, Gil questioned the whereabouts of the others, suggesting they await their return. Stupidly Lance Corporal Weasel insisted and, in a poor imitation of the CSM, using very base vernacular Anglo-Saxon, he barked out his orders. Angry in the extreme, Gil tried to keep his cool and politely requested that the lance corporal speak to him in a civilised manner, but the words fell on deaf ears and Gil was again bluntly ordered to obey the unreasonable task without question.

Oh dear! In the blink of an eye Gil had picked Lance Corporal Weasel up, held him over his head and threw him to the ground. Fortunately for them both, he landed in the V between two metal pickets, from which the barbed wire had been strung and buried as an anchorage point about eighteen inches into the ground. Therefore the lance corporal only sustained minor bruising and shock. Knowing he would limp off to report the incident to the CSM, Gil awaited the fallout, but nothing was either said or done. Obviously the CSM had received another clear message: "Don't mess with me."

There was another twist to all this: some senior NCOs were rarely on site, as most of their time was spent visiting local farmers and the like selling bags of pilfered cement, coils of wire, and anything that could earn them a bob or two. This was common practice, and all the troops knew about it. The sergeant to whom Lance Corporal Weasel would have reported Gil's insubordination was a Scotsman and an active wheeler-dealer who used most of his ill-gotten gains to purchase whisky. In fact, so lucrative was the trade that he was able to invest in enough firewater to become an alcoholic and contract delirium tremens (the DTs), making himself so ill that he was rendered unfit for active service for the rest of the war. Consequently this sergeant was not about to stand before the duty officer reeking of alcohol asking for Gil to be punished.

Of course, the pals relished every opportunity to visit some of the local hostelries – and well deserved too! One particular soirée took Gil and a small group of pals to the Punch Bowl and Ladle public house, just up the road from the King Harry Ferry at Trelissick. Well, he remembers the start of the evening, but having consumed a few too many 'lemonades' the rest of their activities that night are perhaps conveniently forgotten! However, next morning he was told he had enjoyed himself!

That year saw a few more pub crawls across the county, with a couple of jars of local ale here and there. The Cornish proved to be every bit as friendly as the good folk of Yorkshire, so it was rude not too accept their hospitality as well.

True to form, Company Sergeant Major Jennings, who most thought had been thrown out of the Gestapo for being too sadistic, often lived up to his fierce reputation. One night, he caught a hapless group of pals staggering back to camp in the customary intoxicated state, and they were made to sleep it off in some empty dog kennels. Next morning, at the crack of dawn, the 'hangover gang' were made to carry backpacks full of bricks, then march, at double time, up and down a steep hill. It had the desired sobering effect: none of them touched any ale for months, whilst the rest of the company moderated their own future consumption rates.

Chapter X

It was early summer 1941. Their mission to Cornwall complete, 670th Artesian Works Company were posted to Bridestowe, near Okehampton in mid-Devon. For Gil this was tantalisingly close to Beryl and home. The reunited company of sappers set about building yet another Army camp – a routine construction detail for them. It was here that the legendary football match took place, although it, like many others, was more akin to an organised brawl, with some fairly loose bare-knuckle rules.

Summoned to the CO's office at Bridestowe, Gil racked his brains trying to think just what he had done wrong. Then, to his surprise, the Army decided to offer him promotion to lance corporal, a reward for his trade skills and instructional abilities. Taken aback at first, he had no idea they had that much interest in him. Quite naturally he was flattered. Perhaps the company sergeant major liked being shoulder-charged to the ground during football matches? More likely it was Gil's ability to take care of himself physically; the CSM saw something of a kindred spirit in his character and was looking to promote the hard man image. Whatever, Gil decided to politely decline, even though it would have meant extra pay. The officer was somewhat bemused by his rejection, but Gil quickly explained that, as a result of his experiences in France, there was no way he wanted responsibility for the lives of others. He just wanted to look after himself and be one of the boys. The thought of giving the wrong order and causing someone pain or death was too much – he could not do it. He was never offered promotion again.

Gil went home for his next entitlement of ten days' leave, but when Beryl found out he had turned down extra pay she hit the roof. It may not have been much to some, but, when you have nothing to start with, anything is welcome. She was never to forgive him, nor did she understand the principles that led him to make that choice. At that precise moment in time he would have been safer fighting hand-to-hand combat with the Germans than facing the wrath of Beryl. Sixty years later and she would still berate him for it.

But there was some good news for Beryl after all, which probably saved Gil from instant castration. All those recruited as skilled tradesmen, in the belief they would be paid six shillings and sixpence a day, challenged the Army as to why after twenty-one months' service that had not happened. The official reply was that the War Office rules clearly stated that only those who had passed Army trade tests were eligible and only now were they in a position to organise an education programme, which of course they were about to announce! Highly sceptical, Gil signed up for and passed the theory and practical examinations with flying colours and was duly awarded the extra pay so long overdue. That cheered Beryl up, and also saved the painful rearranging of his anatomy!

Gil's tough image was further enhanced at Bridestowe. Whilst being given a haircut in the barrack room and wearing the traditional apron covering from his neck down to his knees, a chap called Dicky Bird pushed his luck just too far and kept lifting the apron up. Funny at first, the repeated interruptions became increasingly annoying to Gil and the barber, both of whom had 'politely' requested Dicky should stop doing it. So on about his tenth apron-lifting mission, and much to his surprise (although if he knew Gil at all he should have anticipated it), Gil stood up and delivered one of his infamous haymakers. The fist caught Dicky square under the chin, and sent him flying through the air. He landed on the floor between two beds, closely followed by an invitation to step outside and settle it once and for all. Dicky sensibly declined the kind offer and backed off, permanently.

Unfortunately Gil was to be a road-accident victim near Bridestowe. He was one of a dozen or so passengers being carried in the back of a lorry negotiating an acute bend, when the driver was confronted by a broken-down lorry just around the blind side of the apex. Being unable to stop, or take evasive action, the two vehicles collided. As a result, six pals, including Gil, sustained heavy impact bruising to their lower backs when knocked to the floor and all ended up being hospitalised in Okehampton. The injury was to permanently weaken Gil's back and return to haunt him some years later.

After just three months, the company was posted to Watchet, near Minehead in Somerset, which geographically was just as temptingly close to home for Gil as Bridestowe had been, but it may as well have been a million miles. With the mood Beryl was in after Gil turned down promotion, it was safer to stay on camp. The Army had commandeered a cliff-top holiday chalet park overlooking the Bristol Channel. The sappers were to build additional accommodation, upgrade the drainage system and transform the civilian park into a military camp. All that took about six months.

You've probably noticed that I've made no mention of Gil's feet since his return from France. That's not to say they were any better – quite the opposite in fact. In France there had been no recourse to sympathetic medical treatment (though, in fairness, he hadn't attempted to obtain any), and in the last weeks of the evacuation only very basic first-aid plasters and bandages were on offer. In Blighty, however, assistance was fairly easy to obtain and, if needed, he asked. Also, the doctors' promises made at both Army medicals when he first joined up of 'suitable work' had come true. The building trade was his favourite line of work, and consequently his dodgy feet were more easily tolerated.

Chapter XI

In early January 1942, Gil and 670th Artesian Works Company were posted to Bicester, in Oxfordshire, where they were to be part of probably the most ambitious engineering project in wartime Britain. This was a building scheme that would take thousands of military and civilian personnel, including prisoners of war, almost three years to complete.

Their task was to build the largest ordnance depot in the British Isles. For Gil this was bliss. It was a project that over time would teach him new skills and test and hone every other trade and skill he had ever been taught, but on a mammoth scale.

The ultimate aim of this colossal depot was to provide a central base, to and from which munitions and equipment would be delivered via a network of new railway lines and roads coming straight into the depot. Also, eight or nine aerodromes in the immediate surrounding countryside would facilitate the swift dispatch of items in support of the Second Front. So the plans were laid for the Allies to retake mainland Europe and the Bicester depot was a major factor in securing that ultimate success.

Gil was amongst the first to arrive on the Oxfordshire site and the initial task, as always, was to build their own barracks with basic facilities and then divide the huge site into work sectors. But long before any heavy construction could begin, or engineering plant be brought into operation, fifteen square miles of wetlands between Bicester, Thane and Aylesbury, had to be drained to provide firm building ground.

Three thousand men at any one time worked around the clock. This included civilians seconded from two building contractors, Wimpy and McAlpines. These men were drafted in to assist five companies of Royal Engineers, together with one company of Mechanical Royal Engineers, one company of Railway Royal Engineers, five companies of Pioneer Corps and four companies of Royal Ordnance Corps.

Tribute must be paid to all those wounded servicemen and disabled people, who volunteered to join rehabilitation companies. These stoic individuals, who had sustained or suffered all manner of incapacity, undertook light tasks befitting their physical status. Some turned out to be highly skilled technicians and tradesmen, but even if the majority were only able to sweep the depot floor, fetch and carry, or other menial jobs, it saved someone else having to do it and played a vital part toward the project staying on track.

After a couple of weeks, Gil and the company were required to undertake annual simulated battlefield training manoeuvres for two weeks, billeted at an RE training camp in the grounds of Shotover House, near Cowley, in Oxfordshire. It was during a cross-country exercise that Gil amazed his pals with the accuracy of his bayonet throwing, winning an extra bob or two on wagers.

The small squad he was in used their initiative to good advantage on one particular night exercise. Whereas everyone else wandered around all night only to end up at the very point they started off from, Gil and his pals found some lorries to sleep under, where they also managed to stay dry.

Meanwhile, out in the darkness, the instructors were setting off firework-type bangers and large thunderflashes to keep the troops on their toes. Little did anyone know, nor did they find out, just what Gil and his pals had achieved. One chap from another team sustained a nasty head wound to his temple when struck by a stone thrown up by one of the bangers. But Gil's team slept through it all.

About two months into the depot project, Gil received the next best thing to a lottery win! When, not by design, his denim overalls became wet, and having taken his boots off to remove the uncomfortable clothing, he trod on a nail, which puncturing deep into the flesh did his already suffering foot no good at all. Finding it difficult to walk forced him to visit the medical reception station, where the duty MO took one look at his dilapidated size-15 plates, admonished him for not coming in sooner, then promised to arranged an appointment for him at the world-famous John Radcliffe Hospital in Oxford. Not only that, but he condemned these sorry feet and issued an official B2 medical grade, which excused Gil from almost every military duty, but allowed him to continue with his trade skills.

Just when he was about to escape from the surgery, thinking that was it, as always in the Army there was a price to pay. This time it came in the shape of a whopping great painful tetanus injection in his stomach that left him feeling very sore. Stepping out into the corridor at just the wrong moment, a rather fat young sapper, whom he had served with at Fowey, in Cornwall, accidentally bumped into him. The pain was excruciating and shot through his body like an electric shock, whereupon Gil did what came naturally to him and delivered one of his infamous haymaker punches square on the fat lad's chin, accompanied by those encouraging words, "You bugger, I'll break your bloody neck!" The fat lad staggered backwards and fell against a wall, but Gil gave him credit for staying on his feet and decided to let it go at that. Quite sensibly the fat lad apologised, about-turned and made a rapid exit.

With so much work to do, time seemed to fly. The days and weeks rapidly turned into months, and all the while Gil's feet were finally starting to cause him serious problems. But despite this he soldiered on. In October the medical officer's promise came good, and Gil was summoned to the John Radcliffe Hospital, where his feet received a thorough examination. The medical board came very close to giving him an immediate medical discharge from the Army, but due to the unique circumstances of the time, his trade skills were considered of great value to the military and he persuaded them to keep him. In truth, civilian wages were probably less than he was receiving from the Army and there was no guarantee of suitable employment outside. He was, however, awarded a new B7 status rendering him almost untouchable. The necessary Army records were updated to confirm all this and he returned to Bicester, where he did what he knew best – construction work.

His lighter duties sometimes included the services of his trusty rifle with fixed bayonet, providing an armed guard over approximately 150 German and Italian prisoners of war, who were usually assigned to trench-digging duties. On one memorable occasion it had started to rain, and the prisoners down in their muddy hole wanted shelter. Gil was having none of that. He had to work in the rain, and so did they. Holding his rifle at the port, diagonally across his chest, he rattled the bolt and fixed them all with his by now infamous 'don't mess with me' stare, together with a few well-chosen Anglo-Saxon verbs, which if shouted loudly enough, seemed to be understood in any language. Wisely they decided to continue working. Make no mistake, more than one would have had to visit the medical officer, and most likely the dentist had they persisted!

With so many men on this huge project, unfortunately, violence and crime was omnipresent. Despite his reputation as a hard man, Gil did his best to avoid confrontation, as the punishments could be pretty dire during wartime when falling foul of King's Regulations, or indeed the civilian criminal law of the day. Of course, for a number of personnel time inside an HMP or military glasshouse was no deterrent. So when a fight broke out at a local dance hall between the sappers and a fearsomely tough assortment of thugs from the Pioneer Corps, quite a few of whom were of Polish descent and all veterans of the Spanish Civil War, renowned for their scant regard for almost any form of authority, chairs and tables flew through the air in all directions. One group stood in the doorway and anyone entering or leaving was hit with a chair! Old and new scores were settled and, from the outset, it soon became obvious the Marquis of Queensberry Rules did not apply. It was strictly gloves-off!

The dance floor apparently resembled an abattoir, being awash with blood, sweat, spit and tears, as well as a few other fluids. It was a pity the RE carpenters didn't think to bring some sawdust with them to soak it up! There were broken teeth, pieces of torn clothing, a million fragments of furniture and broken windows. As one combatant later boasted: "Had it been an Olympic event, artistic and technical merit would have scored a perfect 10." As for why it started – well, rumour said it was all because of a woman. No further comment!

What a sorry bunch appeared on morning parade the next day, when at least twelve sappers each sported an arm in a sling and many others had bruises, cuts, grazes, fat lips, black eyes, lumps and bumps everywhere and chunks missing. There were some with teeth marks! The duty officer gave them a wigging – hurrah! But once he had gone the real bollocking was delivered by the senior NCOs, who made it quite clear, in best blunt Army-style Anglo-Saxon that they were not amused. Privileges were lost and damages started to be deducted from pay. Apart from the physical injuries sustained, which would obviously affect productivity levels for the next couple of days, there was also the substantial compensation claim made against the Army by the dance-hall owner and the likelihood of a police investigation with the threat of criminal prosecutions. But nothing was to hold up the construction project.

Two days later, whether as a result of the dance-hall fight, or something totally unrelated, a sapper was stabbed. He survived, but the civilian police were called to investigate. Gil was in the canteen when the police officers came around showing everyone a knife, purportedly used in the dastardly attack. Gil could tell them nothing. Rumours, however, were rife, but evidence was in short supply and not surprisingly the police drew a blank.

Twelve months had passed and the annual combat refresher training loomed again at Shotover House. This included drill, bayonet practice, shooting and assault courses. Gil with his B7 status was now excused from all this and spent his time helping out in the cookhouse where it wasn't all spud-bashing either. He enjoyed his time there, learnt some basic cooking skills and ate like a lord. It was whilst he was away on this onerous 'eating' course that his son Raymond was born, but regardless he still had to wait his turn for home leave.

Every main building at the new depot was serviced by a circular railway track, controlled from Bicester Station. As soon as a building was declared ready for occupation the trains would steam in with an array of military hardware, including tanks, field guns, bombs, rifles, pistols, ammunition of all calibres, tents, food, spare uniforms (from Savile Row!), jeeps, lorries, motorcycles, small collapsible boats, and hard-tack ration packs. You name it, the list went on and on. The general idea was that when the Second Front had established a foothold in the fight to free mainland Europe, and the first airfield in France was operational, the nine RAF stations surrounding Bicester would receive train and lorry loads of supplies to fly out whatever the troops required. Apparently that is exactly what happened, but by the time it started, Gil had moved on. Job done – his talents were needed elsewhere.

Chapter XII

In March 1943, Gil was posted to 7th Bomb Disposal Company, RE, at Brislington, in Bristol, where for the first few weeks he was based in a small cluster of Nissen huts. After that the troops were moved the short distance to a more permanent Nissen-hut camp in a deer park, just on the outskirts of the city. A busy port since medieval times, Bristol is steeped in engineering history, including those world famous I. K. Brunel creations, the 1843 SS *Great Britain* and the 1853 Clifton Suspension Bridge, both of which survive to this day as testament to his brilliance.

Almost a victim of his own industrious nature, the HQ staff in Bristol were suspicious of Gil's B7 medical grade, and in the May sat him in front of a medical regrading board. Before even looking at his feet, a doctor tried to say he was A1 – typical Army blundering and pig-headedness! When eventually the doctor climbed down off his high horse and actually examined the offending feet and took time to read the report from the esteemed physicians of the John Radcliffe Hospital, there was no argument, just embarrassed shuffling and a swift confirmation of the B7 grade. Not only that, the by now sympathetic doctor said, "If I gave you sandshoes it wouldn't be comfortable, would it?" The board proclaimed that Gil should be issued two pairs of soft black leather civilian boots, because there was no official military footwear considered suitable and they signed a requisition order to that effect.

The very next day, luck was again on his side. With all personnel on parade, the sergeant major called for two volunteers to complete a painting-and-decorating job in a large commandeered house that was to become the company HQ. Together with another chap, Gil was selected for the task. After ten days they finished, resulting in a saving to the company barrack damages fund of over two hundred pounds, a princely sum at that time. The sergeant major was genuinely delighted and personally thanked them both, with the promise of a future favour.

Within days of the medical-regrading-board findings, Gil was being chauffeur-driven on a shopping trip into Bristol city centre by the quartermaster sergeant, a resourceful chap who seemed to know just where to go and who to ask for to get just what was needed. Still, QMs were renown for their ever so slightly dodgy entrepreneurial skills, and Gil decided to play it like the three wise monkeys! Armed with the military requisition order they entered a respectable-looking shoe shop, where, after a professional measuring-and-fitting session the deal was done. The QM handed the requisition order over, probably earning a small remuneration for himself at he same time – and why not?

Gil was well pleased. He knew his feet would not improve, but at least he had two pairs of comfortable, quality-made boots to wear. Remember, B7 medical status affords certain privileges of its own, including being excused drill, parades, guard duty, combat training, etc. However, there were a few ignorant, overzealous NCOs who took a dim view of this and foolishly marched him out for the occasional guard duty. Gil never said a word to them and without argument he would just turn up. It worked every time. They did it to themselves – like pushing a self-destruct button. As soon as the guard commander arrived and recognised Gil with his civilian boots, he would ask the obvious question, and when the magic reply, "B7, sir," was uttered, six lace holes would rapidly disappear up the hapless junior NCO's rear end, much to the delight and mirth of all there.

Gil remained in Bristol for about nine months, working on various jobs, whereupon the sergeant major, true to his word, not forgetting the big favour to company funds those few months before, arranged a plum posting for him. In January 1944 he was sent on secondment as a member of staff to the Royal Engineers bomb recognition and disposal school, situated in the south-coast holiday resort of Bournemouth. He was billeted in a guesthouse, about 150 yards from the school, sharing a bedroom with three other sappers. They also ate all their meals there.

His new job was to assist the teaching staff by constructing practical exercise sites where military personnel, civilian police officers, ARP wardens and the like could practise their bomb-recognition skills and emergency action drills. He also assisted the billeting sergeant with routine administrative chores and escorted students to their quarters – in fact, anything the staff needed help with, he was there. On the 4th April that year, in recognition of time served in the Army, Gil was awarded four inverted service chevrons to be worn at the bottom of his right sleeve.

Meanwhile, during May 1944, Beryl's brother, Arthur, a private in the Devonshire Regiment, was on active service and in the thick of battle at Monte Cassino, Italy, when his parents received one of those dreaded telegrams reporting him 'Killed in action'. This was too much for their mother, who immediately suffered a stroke. It was then expected of Beryl, as she was living with her parents, to look after her mother, which she did willingly. Ironically, as was often the case, another telegram arrived a few days later stating that Arthur was alive, but seriously wounded – all too late for Mother, though!

Monte Cassino had been an architectural treasure and sacred Christian site since the year AD 529. Unfortunately in the hands of the German 4th Parachute Regiment since January 1944, it was a major strength in their defences known as the Gustav Line. The casualty figures on both sides were appalling, with some 105,000 Allied soldiers killed or wounded alongside 80,000 Germans. The Americans took one of the most controversial decisions of the conflict: to bomb the delightful monastery, which was consequently left a shattered wreck and finally fell with heavy casualties to the Polish, assisted by a British contingent.

Gil's one lasting memory of Bournemouth, apart from the parks, gardens and seven miles of beautiful sandy minefield, otherwise known as the beach, was standing in the town centre. It was the 6th June 1944, D-Day, and Operation Overlord, the long-awaited Second Front. Thousands of Allied aircraft flew over, some towing gliders. Wave after wave of them turned the sky black, all making their way toward northern France with a return gift for some of the pain, suffering and destruction unloaded during the Blitz on British cities. Hopefully they were to put an end to Nazi tyranny. It was an awesome sight, and one he often recalls in his mind's eye.

A defeat at this stage could have been a death blow to Britain's war effort, leaving her without an army. General Montgomery commanded 156,000 men, mostly British, American and Canadian troops, of the 21st Army Group, consisting of the British 2nd Army and the US 1st Army, who were to assault the beaches of Normandy between the Orne Estuary and the south-eastern end of the Cotentin Peninsula. Fighting was fierce on all fronts and heavy casualties were sustained. It took until the 20th July before the Allies were able to break out of Normandy and begin the advance through northern France. During all this and long after, the massive supply depot Gil had helped build in Oxfordshire was to play a crucial role.

The German surrender on the 4th May 1945 heralded many joyful celebrations and a gradual programme of demobilisation began, albeit the war in the Far East was to continue until the 14th August.

Gil, meanwhile, was kept on at Bournemouth. Obviously, regardless of where the school was situated, the very nature of their specialised role would gainfully employ the staff, teaching students for years to come the art of clearing minefields and defusing bombs.

He also found himself in charge of the training-school stores, where together with another sapper they were covering the duties of the quartermaster sergeant whilst he was away for a few weeks on a course. With access to anything and everything, they made the most of their time, but remembered to cover their tracks by dealing with the more mundane jobs, such as arranging boot repairs and sorting the laundry orders and returns, creating a persona of efficient military routine.

When the USA detonated two atom bombs on the Japanese cities of Hiroshima and Nagasaki on the 6th and 9th August respectively, Emperor Hirohito overruled his military advisors and, on the 14th August, announced Japan's unconditional surrender. These catastrophic events were to cause major strategy changes to post-war reconstruction plans worldwide.

In late August, Gil was surprised to be told his building talents were required in Germany, and he was to report to the medical centre immediately for mandatory inoculations. He went as ordered, but refused the jabs and when the duty medic insisted, Gil told him in no uncertain terms where to stick his needle! Obviously recognising Gil's sincere intentions, the medic sensibly decided to yield. He never did have them and his pay book was endorsed to that effect in red ink!

Chapter XIII

On the 1st September 1945, following a weekend of home leave, a dozen sappers, including Gil, left Bournemouth by lorry for a brief visit to HQ in Bristol. They then caught a train for Southampton Docks and he had a feeling of déjà vu, when, for the second time he boarded a Channel ferry to Le Havre. His new mission took him to war-ravaged Germany, with orders to help rebuild the basic physical infrastructure, including roads, bridges and the impressive autobahns.

This time he was to ride in a proper railway carriage, which took him east, back through Rouen and the very same countryside he and his comrades had struggled through five years earlier. The stark contrast between the two journeys could not have been more poignant. Yet again he considered fate had been merciful toward him, especially compared to the BEF lads who, for whatever reason, did not make it home in 1940.

The jumping-off point this time was Knokke-Heist, in Belgium. There a transit company was formed, and after two days they moved to yet another camp, this time somewhere in Germany, from where, rather bizarrely, half the men were demobbed and sent home! Gil, however, despite his well-documented B7 disability grading, was retained and mustered into the 555th Field Company, RE, which was put on a train for Dusseldorf, Germany.

On the River Rhine, just outside Dusseldorf, Gil was assigned to a bridging company and placed in charge of a pontoon bridge. Traffic control was essential because the structures were so flimsy, and being only one lane in width, this permitted just three vehicles at a time to cross in any one direction.

One morning, arriving back for another day's duty, the sappers discovered their bridge had taken on a whole new shape. At some time during the night, the notoriously strong Rhine currents had caused one of the mooring anchors to work loose, the rope from which passed through two locking pins with rotating cylinder barrels. One of these pins had been dislodged, resulting in the rope becoming slack and the bridge then bent in the middle, resembling an archer's bow as the fierce current tried to take it all downstream.

Panic was rife amongst the officers, as they anticipated the whole lot disappearing downstream at a rate of knots. A DUKW amphibious landing craft was sent upriver and connected by rope to the centre pontoons, but even with the engine at full power the bridge could not be pulled back into line. Gil took a short walk out along the misshapen construction, but soon decided that this was not such a good idea and returned to firm ground. Eventually, after a full day's sailing, a harbour tug arrived from the docks at Rotterdam, in Holland. That did the job and Gil's bridge was saved.

As a direct result of smuggling and the prolific black market operating throughout Germany, the majority of vehicles, especially lorries, that crossed these temporary bridges were routinely searched. Many a time large piles of contraband could be seen stacked on the roadside, including those most innocuous of objects, potatoes. In towns and cities, during the dead of night, dog carts could be heard trundling along the dark, seemingly deserted streets, and most were allegedly involved in the thriving and, for some, lucrative black market. It was astonishing what some chaps could get for a packet of cigarettes!

For months Gil never drew his pay. All he need do was stand on a street corner, hold up a packet of cigarettes and someone would pay a hundred marks or more. Everyone was doing it. A chap he befriended from the Recce Corps regularly went around with a sack full of coffee, tea, food, and anything he could get his hands on. Every night he would go out armed with a captured German pistol for protection, as some of his exploits and the characters involved sounded decidedly dodgy. Gil, however, had never been a greedy man, so he was quite content with selling enough cigarettes to live comfortably. He even stopped the pub crawls. As long as he had his pipe packed with his favourite ration of tobacco he was happy. His Army pay was held in credit and claimed only after his return to Blighty.

Despite his wonderful civilian boots, Gil's feet were becoming a very real problem, whether at work or leisure, so he reported sick and was given a day off work to attend an Army hospital somewhere in the

Ruhr Valley. Together with a sergeant, he travelled through this area of Germany in the back of a half-track lorry and was speechless most of the way, as mile after mile of totally useless, blitzed, rubble-strewn lunar landscape emerged, with refugees in their own country scrabbling through the debris of what had been people's homes, in a desperate effort to survive. It was pitiful to see.

The Army doctor announced that if his toes were straightened, they would eventually curl back up again, so basically there was nothing he could do for him. 'Tell me something I don't know,' thought Gil, but it had at least given him a day off work.

Even with the monumental task of rebuilding just the basic infrastructure of post-war Germany, life became a touch monotonous for Gil's liking. It was one long round of autobahn rebuilding and Bailey bridge construction, although some permanent bridges were resurrected on their original foundations. His barracks were in old, austere German Army buildings. The window glass had long since been blown out during air raids and Army blankets now plugged the holes. Albeit the weather was mild, there was still an uncomfortable draught whistling through.

The barracks at Dusseldorf were shared, whilst on attachment, with the 1st Battalion, the Welsh Regiment, the ones with a billy goat for a mascot. Fortunately the goat had separate quarters! The consensus opinion was that the Welsh lads, fine fellows though they were, seemed to spend too many hours simply marching up and down – bizarre, when there was so much work to be done. In stark contrast, the sappers laboured around the clock and only used the barracks to sleep in, to register for pay and to eat.

Whilst enjoying a rare moment of rest and relaxation, lounging on their beds one day, who should walk in but Field Marshal Viscount Bernard Montgomery of Alamein, no less. You should have seen those sappers jump. They knew he was visiting the Welsh boys, who had been practising their drill for days and were now lined up outside at an even distance from one another all along the road leading through the camp. What's more, they had also spent hours painting kerbstones white and polishing everything else, including their billy goat. The very last thing the REs expected was a barrack-room inspection.

Wearing only work fatigues and playing cards, some of the lads were immediately placed on a charge. Gil protested his innocence and, by some fluke, convinced the Welsh RSM he was resting his B7 feet, so he narrowly escaped punishment. By all accounts Monty was not amused, but then he wasn't known for his humour or benevolence. However, he was impressed with the Welsh boys' bullshit. Even the shiny billy goat won an extra carrot.

On the 3rd January 1946, whilst still serving with 555th Field Company, RE, at Dusseldorf, Gil at last received his Army-release leave certificate, form X 202/A, upon which an RE captain, whom he had never met, endorsed Gil's military conduct as 'exemplary' with a testimonial stating, 'This man is a smart and competent worker and can be relied upon to carry out his duties efficiently. He is tactful and sober and thoroughly trustworthy and reliable.' Well, who could, or in their right mind would, argue with that? Back in Brighton, at the RE Records Office, Army form X 202/B was generated, this being a certificate of transfer to the Army reserve list, which would officially expire on the 12th March 1946. He still has a copy of both forms.

Having returned to Blighty, again courtesy of a Channel ferry to Southampton, Gil reported to a demob centre set up at an Army camp in Taunton, Somerset, and, on the 7th January, after an overnight stay, a forest of forms was signed and stamped. He then handed over all items of uniform, together with his faithful old 1914 rifle with the dodgy safety catch and his pocket-money-earning bayonet, in exchange for three medals – the 1939–45 Star, the Defence Medal and the War Medal – all his owed back pay, a civilian suit and a rail warrant. His Army service had commenced on the 11th January 1940 and officially ended on the 11th March 1946, as attested to on his Army Record of Service card, form W5258.

With mixed emotions, which included the excitement of opportunity that peace brought, but equally the trepidation of securing employment to support his family (where and how were they to live?), he boarded a train at Taunton, which in those days had a direct line to Barnstaple. He arrived home to a warm reunion with his wife and child, who unfortunately were still residing under very strained conditions with her parents. Due to a lack of either affordable housing, or council accommodation, they were to remain there for another seven years.

Finding employment back on Civvy Street was frustrating. The world had changed, and some people appeared indifferent to the sacrifice and suffering endured by ex-service personnel. There were no automatic jobs for the boys, no helping hands from a grateful nation. Some had been traumatised by their experiences, and wounds could be both physical and psychological, but the general attitude was 'bite the bullet and get on with it', especially from those who had managed to lead a charmed life in uniform, or did not serve the colours and contributed little or nothing to the war effort.

Eventually, after seven long years and the surprise of Beryl falling pregnant again, they started looking for a place of their own. On hearing this, Beryl's father immediately and heartlessly ordered them out of his house, choosing to forget the sacrifices they had already made in caring for her mother. Beryl's father had always been a difficult man, a heavy drinker and a tough North Devonian character who thought and negotiated with his fists. He had regularly threatened to throw them out of the house, but this time he meant it.

With just a few hours' notice to quit, they moved in with Gil's parents in Braunton. Yet more strained relationships developed there, as many families discover when living with relatives, but with little in the way of savings what else was there to do?

After six months, with nerves at breaking point and the pregnancy well advanced, they received the invaluable assistance of their sympathetic GP, Doctor Barlow, who provided enough evidence for them to be awarded a council house on the Forches Estate in Barnstaple.

Shortly after arriving there, in 1954, their daughter Carol was born. Many a tale can be told of the continuing struggle to make ends meet, and the characters, both helpful and not so, who shaped their new world. But at least now they were independent.

Sadly, albeit a merciful release, Beryl's mother passed away; and family life took another twist in 1960, when her father died. As fate would have it, at that same time Gil was offered compensation following an industrial accident sustained whilst overreaching on a building site. He had fallen and spent weeks in hospital and a further six months in a plaster-cast jacket. He was awarded either a life pension or a lump sum. The chance of purchasing the old family home made that choice easy, so they took over the mortgage and progressed to become house owners at last in Higher Maudlin Street, Barnstaple.

During the next thirty years, prior to taking early retirement, Gil plied his masterly building skills between various employers in the North Devon area, including Hammett & Diamond, Goviers and latterly Woolaways, being heavily involved in the post-war construction and repair of literally hundreds of dwellings and businesses in North Devon. His work is still providing homes for thousands of people. He continued until his back finally gave up, which put an end to any heavy work and he spent the last few working years at the DeVere factory on the Pottington Industrial Estate, Barnstaple, making precision camera parts.

Despite the struggle to make ends meet, necessitating both of them doing two jobs each whilst raising two children and running a house, Beryl and Gil have always stood by each other and now, most deservedly, live comfortably in a smart new Methodist Homes flat in the centre of Barnstaple. Here they still enjoy their independence, whilst under the watchful stewardship of the scheme manager, her staff and, most importantly, the attentive care of their daughter Carol.

Of the original seven North Devon pals who enlisted into the Royal Engineers at Barnstaple on that fateful day back in December 1939, all somehow managed to survive the war. Sadly, though, sixty years on and beyond his ninetieth year, Gil is now the lone survivor.

Tribute: The Royal Engineers

William the Conqueror landed on our shores in 1066. Amongst the army entourage was his very own 'King's Engineer' and for hundreds of years thereafter a succession of noblemen bore the title. These men were responsible for a huge variety of both military and civilian construction on the British Isles, with a tendency toward coastal defences, especially during the reign of Henry VIII. Defensive earthworks were already well developed by the second millennium BC, with plenty of examples worldwide proving the importance of the engineer, which has long been recognised by numerous civilisations.

By the end of the Middle Ages the art of the military engineer had become an integral part of the British military establishment. With the invention of gunpowder in the 14th century, warfare had been reduced to a series of sieges of well-protected fortresses. This in turn led to the engineers' nickname of sappers, derived from the application of geometry and a zigzag form of approach trench known as a sap, dug toward the walls of a besieged fortress so as not to expose troops to hostile fire. Undermining the walls also became an important new task for military engineers.

Thus the digger of a sap became a sapper and the name stuck. The present Corps of Royal Engineers officially started in 1716 when George I issued a royal warrant to establish a Corps of Engineers and the Royal Regiment of Artillery, both under the control of the Board of Ordnance. To this day the Engineers and the Gunners share the same regimental colours of dark blue and red.

The initial establishment of the new Corps of Engineers was of only twenty-eight officers. For their labour force they had to rely upon civilians and it remained that way until 1772 when the first Soldier

74

Artificer Company was formed in Gibraltar, later expanding by 1787 to six companies and commanded by Royal Engineer officers. As British interests expanded in the 17th century and her soldiers were spread around the world, the engineers went with them. Specialist companies were established in countries including India and Canada. Several campaigns later, in 1797, the Corps was granted the title of Royal thus becoming the Corps of Royal Engineers.

During the Napoleonic Wars the officer cadre of the Royal Engineers made their greatest impact in the Peninsular Campaigns, where their fortunes varied from the desperate assaults on Badajoz, to the tremendous effort in the construction of the defensive line at Torres Vedras, which saved Lisbon. Hailed as one of the major feats of military engineering of the era, it was completed almost entirely by civilian labour under the guidance of the Royal Engineers and Royal Military Artificers.

In 1812, partly due to the recommendation of the Duke of Wellington, the Artificers became the Royal Sappers. The Board of Ordnance was finally abolished in 1855. The following year the Sappers were united with the Engineers to become the Corps of Royal Engineers and at long last the officers of the Corps had direct command of the men whom they had usually called upon to implement their various projects.

The Royal Engineers have always been special. Soldiers who enter the ranks of the sappers usually do so with a sense of vocation and ambition. From these ranks have emerged a disproportionately high number of top commanders, some of the most powerful and remarkable men in the British Army, who have influenced both military and civilian life. The amalgamation in 1862 with elements of the old East India Company, who had run its own private army complete with staff college and an engineer arm every bit as proficient as the Royal Engineers, provided yet more personnel of high calibre. This was brought about by colonial campaigns and the influence of notable characters. Perhaps the most important of them, and an engineer revered to this day, was Field Marshal Earl Horatio Kitchener of Khartoum, who started life as a sapper and later became the best known soldier of his generation. As Secretary of War his face dominated recruiting posters during the First World War and he is accredited with recruiting 3,000,000 volunteers for the armed services.

The Corps has been involved in every bush war and colonial campaign fought by the British Army. The most famous must be the Zulu War saga of Rorke's Drift, where, heavily outnumbered, the British defenders were led by one Lieutenant Chard, a Royal Engineer officer commanding a ferry. His richly deserved Victoria Cross was but one of many won by sappers.

Throughout history, with each new technological breakthrough, sappers were usually involved and over the centuries a vast array of specialist companies and independent corps have been formed. The Industrial Revolution of the mid-Victorian period up to the end of the First World War saw an era of vast industrial and social change, highlighting the Corps' ability to adapt and diversify, and their obvious influence on the modern military organisation, including the following: railway/harbour/docks/bridge construction; telegraph; submarine mining; fortress and defence electric lights; mounted troops; the balloon school at Chatham, which became the Royal Flying Corps and by 1918 evolved into the Royal Air Force and Fleet Air Arm; the Steam Road Traction Unit, which became the Army Service Corps then the Royal Corps of Transport and now the Royal Logistic Corps; tunnelling; forestry; surveying to produce maps; artisan works; well-boring; land drainage; road construction; quarrying and a war dogs' school. Chemical warfare saw Sapper Livens give his name to a projector used to fire chemical canisters; Sapper Nissen gave his name to the famous design of hut; the flame-thrower was a sapper innovation from a German model; and the first tank corps was commanded by a sapper.

A Postal Section provided postal support to the Army during both world wars, albeit the origins date back to 1799.

With the end of the First World War the Corps and its myriad of companies and units shrank back to pre-war size, handing over responsibility for a whole range of tasks to other corps. Life for the Royal Engineers was seldom dull during the inter-war years, with sappers around the world being gainfully employed.

By the time the Second World War started, the Corps was fully mechanised and for the first time when they went to France they did so without the horse. The scope of RE activity had always been diverse but during the Second World War it was immense. New duties led to new sapper units being formed, including those for the disposal of unexploded bombs and those of assault engineers, who used suitably modified tanks and new armoured amphibious vehicles to lead an attack and clear the way, taking out strongpoints and defended positions. Also mine-clearance units using mechanical devices such as ploughs, flails and rollers were formed. Other new items of equipment had to be mastered, including the Bailey bridge, an array of demolition devices, assault boats and pontoons for river crossings.

Royal Engineers have fought and will continue to fight and work anywhere they are needed. The old cry of 'Call for the sappers' was heard in all corners of the globe both on the front line and just as importantly behind the lines, helping the Army to move, fight and survive. They supplied water and electricity, ran the railways and operated the docks, laying barbed wire, building pillboxes and excavating bombproof shelters. Their assault bridges often remained in place for months until substantial construction work could commence. They built and repaired airfields and landing strips for the RAF. They cleared minefields, especially in North Africa, and led the way ashore during the Normandy Landings of June 1944 and the subsequent move inland.

Combat Engineer Airborne Units saw action on Sicily in 1943 and again during the Normandy Landings. Building and maintaining the Rhine crossings enabled the Allies to move freely across Germany to secure peace. In the Far East, working with the Indian engineers to fight the Burma Campaign, where sappers toiled in the dreadful tropical climate and environment, it was no terrain for the internal combustion engine so mules or buffaloes were all that could be used on land, with river supply routes playing a major role.

Over the last one thousand years Royal Engineers have carried out their diverse professional tasks to the benefit of both military and civilian objectives. Performing many services for communities throughout the world, sappers have built roads and bridges, supplied water and electricity, carried out surveys, produced maps, constructed public buildings and utilities of all kinds, and provided relief operations following natural disasters, making the difference between life and death whilst winning hearts and minds.

The modern 21st-century sapper is first trained as a soldier, then as a combat engineer and finally as a tradesman, choosing from a comprehensive range of trades including, communications, driver, electrician, general fitter, draughtsman (electrical and mechanical), surveyor, bricklayer, building finisher, fitter (air conditioning and refrigeration), plumber, materials technician, data technician, carpenter, fabricator, plant operator, design draughtsman (buildings and engineer structures), and production technician (map-maker). In addition, there is an opportunity to train in one of the specialist roles, which include RE Commando (working alongside the Royal Marines and wearing the coveted green beret), Paratrooper, Airborne Sapper (working alongside the Parachute Regiment and wearing the much prized maroon beret), RE Diver, (commercially trained), Bomb Disposal, and Armoured and Amphibious Engineers.

There are now five Army corps offering a huge variety of either new or inherited engineering trades, including the Royal Engineers, the Royal Electrical and Mechanical Engineers, the Royal Signals, the Royal Logistic Corps and the Army Air Corps.

Although that bruising soccer match at Bridestowe back in 1941 was more about brawn than skill, the Corps has maintained a fine sporting tradition, including winning the FA Cup in 1875. Had Gil been in the team he would probably have received the very first red card.

Sapper 1910766 Gilbert James Mock is proud to have served with the Royal Engineers, even though for most of the time his feet hurt!